T0375594

HELLO, MY NAME IS

Grace

THE RETURN OF YESHUA/JESUS

GRACE SHEPHERD

WESTBOW
P R E S S®
A DIVISION OF THOMAS NELSON
& ZONDERVAN

WestBow Press books may be ordered through booksellers or by contacting:

WestBow Press
A Division of Thomas Nelson & Zondervan
1663 Liberty Drive
Bloomington, IN 47403
www.westbowpress.com
844-714-3454

ISBN: 979-8-3850-3479-6 (sc)
ISBN: 979-8-3850-3480-2 (hc)
ISBN: 979-8-3850-3481-9 (e)

Library of Congress Control Number: 2024920422

Print information available on the last page.

WestBow Press rev. date: 11/25/2024

With a grateful heart, I would like to thank the following people. This manuscript would not have been possible without the loving support of my life partner. She has, over the many years of us being paired together, both held me tight and let me go as I needed. I am truly grateful for her and the many friends who have embraced and encouraged me along this journey. I would like to give a special thank-you to Jo-Ann, who was brave and kind enough to edit these pages and fine-tune what I wanted to say.

My heartfelt appreciation goes out to the present and past ministers at my childhood church; they both reviewed my story for scriptural and factual accuracy and offered their valuable insights. Also, I am grateful to my Sanctuary Book Club friends, especially to Jane V., who welcomed me into the group and week after week helped me to come out of my shell and provide a safe space to share my thoughts and feelings. Thank you to my family, who gave me the foundation to become who I am, but most of all, *thank you to the Creator*, who holds us all by the hand and helps us along the way.

It is my pleasure to acknowledge Deb Blanchard of TAC—The Adoption Connection. She is a crusader for all the members of the adoption triad and has been successful in her campaigns to open birth records. Deb helped me to find my birth mother and held support-group meetings in public places as well as in her very home. These meetings gave me the love and understanding that I needed throughout my reunion experience. I had been one of the members that she had asked to write a chapter for her memoir: *Love Never Leaves*. Check it out; it's truly inspirational, especially for those who have struggled with racial issues. From that invitation to write just one small chapter came the seed of inspiration and encouragement that I needed to put my story down on paper. It is with gratitude that I share all of this. My hope is that you, the reader, might find your own inspiration and encouragement within these pages.

Contents

Preface

This is my story, but it is not about me. As you might image by the title, this is a book about grace—God's grace. Oftentimes people think of *grace* as being God's unmerited favor—a free pass on our sins, if you will. While this is true, to a degree, it is so much more than that. The dictionary defines *grace* as "courteous goodwill, simple elegance, or refinement of movement."

I like the third idea: "refinement of movement." It conjures up images of living life in a way that is nonabrasive—kind, gentle, and caring. It brings to mind the fruits of the Spirit, which are found in Galatians 5:22–23 (NLV): "Love, joy, peace, patience, kindness, goodness, faithfulness, gentleness, and self-control." These are in the very image of our Creator, but these "fruits" can only come into existence in a person's soul through the crucifixion of the flesh. What is meant by that can be found in the twenty-fourth verse of Galatians, which tells us that "those who belong to Christ Jesus have crucified the flesh with its passions and desires." James 4 strongly encourages us to humble ourselves. Isn't it ironic that we are only truly alive when we finally "die to self"? When we learn to trust God and are reborn in the Spirit, that's when we discover divine grace. *Wikipedia* defines *divine grace* as "a theological term present in many religions. It has been defined as the divine influence which operates in humans to regenerate and sanctify, to inspire virtuous impulses, and impart strength to endure trials and resist temptation; and as an individual virtue or excellence of divine origin." For me, this raises the question of my origin. As an adoptee, these things often stir my sense of curiosity, and I once again start wondering. Where did I come from, where did we come from, why are we here, and where is this story called life leading us?

As you will see in the theme of these pages, grace is the glue that holds us and the universe together. It holds our individual bodies together through *laminin*, a cell-adhesion molecule that interestingly is in the shape of the cross (seriously, google it), and it holds the body of Christ, the church, together when we learn to trust, surrender to, and cooperate with our Creator. We learn obedience through trust, not intimidation. When God finally has His way, we all win!

I would like to share with you my experience of divine grace in the hope that you might find strength and comfort in the storms of life. I hope that Christ will strengthen you in your inner being (Ephesians 3:16 NIV) as you walk with me through these pages. Hope is the light that shines in the darkness of doubt and fear. When we share our stories and reveal our secrets, we connect in genuine and authentic ways, and our communities are strengthened. This is my journey from being worthless in the world to becoming worthy in Christ. What you are about to read might be disturbing to some and seem far-fetched to others. I have been told that my story reads like fiction. Quite honestly, if I had not experienced these things and had other people to witness them and validate me, I would think the same. I assure you that to the best of my recollection, these events are true.

Chapter 1

WHO, WHAT, WHERE, AND WHY?

Who are you? A child of God.

What does this mean? We are called to share our gifts and talents.

Where is your treasure? What matters most to you? Heaven.

"For where your treasure is, there your heart will be also" (Matthew 6:21 NRSV).

Why are you here? To love and serve God, as well as my neighbor and even my enemies.

LET ME INTRODUCE myself. My legal name is a variant of *Nanette,* but I have chosen to keep private my given name at the time of my adoption out of respect for the people mentioned within these pages. My parents adopted me as an infant and named me this because it was my mom's favorite name. I believe she saved this name for me because the Holy Spirit inspired her to do so. After reading this story, let's see if you will agree! As a child, I didn't really have any set nicknames per se. My mother's sister, my aunt, called me Nanny-goat, and a grade-school friend would sometimes call me Beggar, but that's about it. *Beggar*, as I later learned, is actually a great depiction of our reality as Christians, but as a kid, I always thought it was kind of mean for this girl to call me that. I wonder now why I kept her as a friend. I liked *Nanny-goat* because of its association with being sure-footed.

I was born in April in the early 1960s in Boston City Hospital to an unwed mother. I have no idea who was present at my birth, but I imagine there were many angels in the room to help deliver me. I do have some nonidentifying information that was passed along to my adoptive parents, and there is evidence that there was much distress at the time of my birth. I entered the foster-care system immediately. I was placed for adoption at a little over six months of age. In my new family, I was the youngest of four; in comparison, my eldest brother was nine years older, my sister was seven years older, and my other brother was five years older than me.

My childhood home was in the suburbs south of Boston, and my family moved farther south to a larger home when I was about two and a half years old. I don't remember the first house, but my parents stayed in the house that I grew up in until they moved into assisted living. This happened long after my siblings and I were grown adults and living on our own. As a young girl, I shared a room with my older sister; but when she went to college, I had the room to myself. My mom helped me to redecorate it, and I chose pink-and-light-green flowered wallpaper that had a striped pattern. The trim was painted light green, and the curtains were white with a hint of lace on the edges. The color scheme was pleasant, and it made me happy. The only thing I didn't like was the angled wall at the front of the house because it made it hard to decorate. From that house, I moved many, many times, but it was always temporary, and I frequently landed back at my parent's home to re-center myself. Eventually, I moved into my paternal grandparents' house in Plymouth, Massachusetts, after they had passed away. That house was haunted by them, and I absolutely loved the fact that their spirits were there. I never felt alone, and I knew they were there to protect me. Many of my friends who visited me got creeped out in my house if they were there alone, but they were fine if I was in the house with them. At one point, I had a malicious roommate whom I struggled to evict, but my nana's ghost scared him away. Thank God! From there, I met my life partner and moved to the town right next to the one I grew up in, and I still live there now—more than thirty years later.

WHO'S YOUR DADDY?

The man who adopted me was born in the early 1920s, which made him a full forty years older than I was. He was a handsome man; he was five feet eight and had brown hair and hazel eyes. He was raised in the suburbs south of Boston and was baptized in April 1928 at a Congregational church in the same town where he attended high school. Dad was a college graduate, but he completed his degree by attending night school after marrying my mom in 1946. At one time, he had worked at a drugstore as a soda jerk. He always seemed to light up when he told stories about his time there, and I would venture to guess that it was his favorite job. He was certified in blueprint reading for ship workers, following in his father's footsteps to become a draftsman. Dad's long-term career was where he had a supportive boss and at least one dear friend who, incidentally, lived next door to the woman I would one day marry. My grandfather did go on to become an architect, but Dad was never overly ambitious or anxious to advance at work because he always put his family first. He *never* missed any of my softball games. When I run into old friends with whom I played ball, they always remember my dad as a spectator sitting in his red canvas folding chair. I still have that chair.

My father was always very personable and well-liked by

everyone. Often, folks would refer to him as the mayor of wherever he was affiliated. He could be a bit bullheaded, and I believe I inherited that trait from him. I believe that I have refined that characteristic, and thankfully, I keep to just being tenacious (most of the time). Dad had a strong underlying religious base, but his faith sometimes wavered when it was challenged by his obedience to my mother. She always ruled the roost, and I often wished he would stand up to her. He did this in a passive way by slipping me money at times to pursue things that he approved of me doing even if she was not quite on board. My relationship with my dad was very good while I was growing up. He taught me to ride a bike, throw a ball, drive, be a person of my word, and always be on time (he was a stickler on that one). He taught my siblings and me so many wonderful things. The summer of 1985 changed the dynamics of our relationship, but I will talk about that later.

Both of my parents enjoyed the outdoors; they loved camping, gardening, and even skiing with my mother's sister in New Hampshire when they were younger. Mom was an avid reader, but Dad preferred to work with his hands in his spare time. They both liked to play card games with family and friends. I remember many potluck dinners and rousing games with spirited conversations. My siblings and I could use language during card games that we would otherwise have our mouths washed with soap for. Dad had a standing cribbage game with our next-door neighbor where they wagered a small amount of money, and whenever the pool was enough, they would take the wives out for dinner. These and many others are all such fond memories.

MOM

My mother—what can I say about Mom? We had a complicated relationship, that's for sure. She met my dad in the youth group at the local church where she had been baptized in January 1933. Mom was forgiving—I know because my dad had stood her up on their first date. He was supposed to take her to a concert but left her standing on a street corner. He made it up to her, and the rest is history. She was born in Boston and raised in Quincy, the birthplace of John Quincy Adams. When I was a child, she took me and the Girl Scout group that she led to the Adams homestead. While we were touring his house, the curator let me sit in the chair that was once JQA's when he was a boy. It brought joy to my mom to see me in that little seat that had belonged to someone so influential and honored. Regarding her own family, Mom had one older sister who was close in age to her, one much younger than her, and two younger brothers. Her younger sister, still living at the time of this writing, remembers very little of my mom growing up, but she shared stories of how they moved to a house on a lake. She remembered that they had to use Ivory soap (which floated) when they bathed in the lake. Money was tight, and they couldn't afford to lose the bar. There are stories of the meager meals they would enjoy, like sugar sandwiches and warm milk with cinnamon over macaroni. These events happened during the Great Depression.

Mom had a rough time when she was young. Her parents were German immigrants, and her mom barely spoke English. When she was just seventeen years old, her dad died suddenly of a heart attack. As she was the second oldest in her family and her older sister was quite timid, she was thrust into the position of head of the household. This molded her, forcing her to be fiercely strong in character. I can't image what it was like for her to be the family's provider in an era when women were still seen as objects for men's pleasure. I imagine that she must have been put in many compromising situations that she was unable to escape because of her responsibilities to her family. I both admire her resilience and hate what it did to her. My mom was extremely loving, but I felt that there was always a string attached. The price was to give her control. I don't blame her one bit, but me being me, I needed to rebel.

Mom was very intelligent and mastered all her math courses in grade school very early. The story goes that they ran out of teachers who could educate her past the level she had achieved. I often wonder how differently her path might have been academically and professionally had she been a man. At one time, she worked where my dad also worked, but most of her career involved teaching kindergarten. She obtained a day-care license in May 1975 after completing her course work in achieving development in young children. Perhaps this career choice helped her to grow emotionally. Her intelligence was a blessing, but it also enabled her to become very manipulative. We were more alike than I care to admit. Thankfully, I think I have been able to shed some of her negative characteristics; at the very least, I am sure that I am more aware of them and try to keep them in check.

After many years of wrestling with my relationship with her, I am most grateful that she taught me to love God and to seek His ways. If not for that, I would most likely be bitter and have remained unable to truly love. I did love my mom—deeply. I still have the sweaters she knitted for me and visit her and my dad's graves on a regular basis. Being the youngest of four and adopted, I was like an only child in my relationship with her in many ways. We had many special adventures together. Some of my favorite memories are of our trips to have lunch at the Strawberry Fair. At the time, it was a restaurant for ladies only, and I thought that was super cool. She also enjoyed clothes shopping and loved to buy me things that I would never have bought for myself. So, with all my mixed feelings, it makes me ask this: *How do we categorize people as either good or bad?* This question became *very* pertinent during my search for my birth mother. People often ignore the basic need to know where we came from, and they would ask me why I was even searching. They even asked me if it was because I had bad adoptive parents. I won't get into how misguided that question is; that's another book in and of itself. Suffice it to say, my search had very little to do with who adopted me or my happiness with my adoptive family.

One thing worth mentioning here is what had preoccupied her attention in her final days. I had asked the pastor of the church I was raised in to visit my parents and help them prepare for the inevitable. They were both in hospice care and were struggling to reconcile everything. My dad was outright afraid to die for fear of punishment that he thought he had coming to him. The pastoral visits did help tremendously. On the last visit before Mom died, the pastor shared with me that she refused communion. That was *completely* out of character for her. I asked him why, and he said that she was intent on watching the show that was on TV. After I was prompted by the Holy Spirit to ask for the name of the show, he shared that it was *Dr. Phil,* but he had no idea what the subject matter was. I left it alone and forgot about it for a while. Then another instance of prompting caused me to realize that I knew what the date of the visit was and could simply look up what the program was about that day. It was about mothers who had tried to kill their infant children. Very interesting, to say the least, and this information was key in discovering my true identity.

INTRINSICALLY GOOD OR EVIL?

There is an age-old debate as to whether we are born basically good or if we are born with original sin. I believe that we are born selfish and needy in nature, expecting those needs to be fulfilled with no regard or understanding of the pressures that are put on those who fill those needs, including and especially the pressures put upon our parents and other family members. We grow up in environments with people who have various degrees of spiritual maturity as well as various degrees of brokenness, and we tend to emulate those behaviors. This process is carried out by the scripts that are written for us by those who raised us as well as what we inherited through DNA. If we are not mindful, we will run on autopilot until some trauma wakes us from our unconscious state and begs us to look upward. It will ask us to look to something bigger than ourselves to fulfill our needs and to emulate the behaviors of our Creator, who is self-actualized. The journey takes a lifetime and is never actually completed until we cease to live in this realm. But seeking continuous improvement, especially in the spiritual sense, is what keeps life interesting and worth living.

Along this journey, as with any good drama, there are obstacles and challenges. We are in a virtual battleground and need to be prepared. *Step number one: Know your enemy!* I used to think that my enemy was whoever was standing in opposition to me at the moment, but I have come to realize that there is a pattern in all my encounters. The most consistent thing in all my problems was the obvious common denominator: me! I was—and sometimes still am—my own worst enemy. But more than that, what is it within me that makes this so? This chapter is about the who, what, where, and why of it all. The child inside wants *more* answers, and so I would like to expound upon the why:

> Why are you here? To love and serve God—the Almighty Creator, my neighbor, *and* my enemy. *But first, you must learn to love yourself.*
> Why? Because the Almighty Creator loves and serves me (us).
> Why? Because the Almighty Creator is relentlessly, tenaciously in love with us.
> Why? Because that is the Almighty Creator's nature. Because we are His/Her creation, we *are* lovable.

Why? Because we were created to be in a state of relationship. The Almighty Creator wants to bring us to full maturity and then marry us. Why? Because love always wins!

But let's go back to the battle story in front of us. We do have work to do, and we need to have the right tools, so put on your armor and walk with me through the story of how I went from feeling unworthy to realizing that we are all beloved—even me.

Here's your outfit for the journey: Ephesians 6:10–17 (NIV).

The Armor of God

Finally, be strong in the LORD and in his mighty power. Put on the full armor of God, so that you can take your stand against the devil's schemes. For our struggle is not against flesh and blood, but against the rulers, against the authorities, against the powers of this dark world, and against the spiritual forces of evil in the heavenly realms. Therefore, put on the full armor of God, so that when the day of evil comes, you may be able to stand your ground, and after you have done everything, to stand. Stand firm then, with the belt of truth buckled around your waist, with the breastplate of righteousness in place, and with your feet fitted with the readiness that comes from the gospel of peace. In addition to all this, take up the shield of faith, with which you can extinguish all the flaming arrows of the evil one. Take the helmet of salvation and the sword of the Spirit, which is the word of God.

Chapter 2

SECRET, SECRET

IN THE PAGES of this chapter, I have chosen to write in third-person prose because it is far too painful to write freely in the first person. I will step back and narrate my story as if I were a bystander but one with intimate knowledge of the character. This is in line with the fact that I suffered from episodes of disassociation during this time of my life. I would occasionally be in my body but also outside my body, floating along and noticing my interactions and awkwardness in social situations. In the following chapters, I will return to first-person accounts of my story. I will do this for His glory, turning my mess into His message. As I was being nudged awake by God to discover the hidden things of my family dynamics, the name Lisa was used to help me identify hard truths, so in this chapter, I will refer to myself as Lisa.

This is the story of a girl who was born unwanted and made to feel unworthy of love. She was not named at birth because she was a "mistake." From the point of conception, her existence was threatening to others—threatening not just to the birth mother and the birth father, whose identities may someday be exposed, but to all who live in darkness and choose to cling to evil because she was born to speak truth to power. The rulers, authorities, and principalities of this world and the cosmic powers and spiritual forces of evil in the heavenly places that are spoken of in Ephesians 6:12 have every reason to fear when Lisa grows to full maturity. The core force of evil that caused her birth mother's pregnancy is in jeopardy of losing influence and control. There will be an end to patriarchy and the abuse of authority. The scriptures promise this, and you can bet your donkey (ass) that this little "reject" will grow up into the fullness of Christ!

The alleged act of violence that caused the conception of Lisa and the ensuing pregnancy were almost more than her birth mother could bear. Yet God gives more grace in these times of darkness. For the sake of this story, we will call the birth mother Belle because it suits her personality. She was always the belle of the ball. A lifetime of dysfunction and unhealthy coping mechanisms caused untold emotional, spiritual, and physical damage to Belle, and now it was being passed on to an unintended victim—Lisa, the child who was born. Unable to give this child what she needed, Belle chose to relinquish her. She was placed into a foster home and later adopted by a well-intentioned family.

Psalm 51:5–6 (NIV) says, "Surely, I was sinful at birth, sinful from the time my mother conceived me. Yet you desired faithfulness even in the womb; you taught me wisdom in that secret place."

Those verses are a powerful reminder that, as the Quest Study Bible says in the margin of this passage, "the reality of our sin should prevent us from becoming complacent or proud. We inherit our sinful nature from our earthly parents, but our Divine nature from our Heavenly one."

After the adoption, the records were sealed, leaving Lisa to wonder who her earthly bloodline parents were. She was so young, and already there were so many secrets. Very little information was passed along at the time of the adoption, but Lisa's nonidentifying birth records showed that at her birth, the umbilical cord was green—a true sign of the toxicity that Lisa would need to overcome if she would ever learn to thrive.

Most, but not all, secrets are toxic. For instance, when God keeps things from us, it's always for our ultimate good. We find just such an example in Colossians 1:26–29 (BBE):

> The secret which has been kept from all times and generations, but now been made clear to his saints, To whom God was pleased to give

knowledge of the wealth of the glory of this secret among the Gentiles, which is Christ in you, the hope of glory: Whom we are preaching; guiding and teaching every man [*person*] in all wisdom, so that every man [*person*] may be complete in Christ; And for this purpose I am working, using all my strength by the help of his power which is working in me strongly.

In other words, there will come a time when we need to grow into full maturity. God will only keep us in the dark for a period of time, and He does this to protect us until we are able to understand. The following story is how that happened to Lisa.

The phone rang, and it was social services asking a couple who had already adopted several other children to take in one more. Their first response was to say no; their finances were already spread too thin, and their small house just didn't have enough room for any addition to the family. The folks at the adoption agency urged them to reconsider and offered to waive all legal and processing fees. They could have the child for free. Seven months later, the adoption took place, and one year and one day later, it was finalized. She was legally their child. Little did they know that this decision would cost them in ways that can't be measured in any tangible way. This little girl was sent there to not only change the trajectory of the child's life but also to change the family, and through the ripple effect of the adoption, countless other lives were changed as well. As I reflect on the stories of Simeon and Moses, it occurs to me that God has a way of using innocent babies, the least likely agents, to do His "dirty work." God always seems to heal us by allowing major shifts in our lives. He nudges us out of our comfort zones and into His promises.

Change can be difficult. The first major thing was that Lisa's new family needed to relocate. They needed a bigger house, but the money was tight. Luckily, or perhaps by divine providence, the adoptive mother had a brother who happened to be a builder. He had dropped out of school when he was a boy because he had dyslexia during a time when it was not yet understood; his teachers thought he was unintelligent because of their ignorance. There were five siblings in all (as mentioned in chapter 1), and they had lost their father to a heart attack. I suppose that dropping out of school seemed to be the right thing to do at the time. However, he was not without intelligence as they had supposed—far from it. In fact, he became not just a builder but a very successful and wealthy master builder who was renowned for his craftsmanship. By the time his sister had adopted Lisa and needed to move, he owned a large amount of land, so he built the family a new house. It was a lovely home, but it came with some added stress. Because of the location, a second car was needed. The other siblings had to leave all their friends behind. The community support they were used to—their network of neighbors—was left behind, and this created a void at the new house. There was also the matter of finding a new church to attend. That church would one day reject Lisa, but more will be said about that later. Suffice it to say, all the challenges gave the family more opportunities for growth. As for Lisa, as she grew, she was always presented with the choice to either implode/self-destruct or take the other path and conquer the biggest hurdle of all—learning to "forgive" God for all the pain. We know that God does no wrong and never requires forgiveness, but she needed to discover this for herself and realize who God really is.

The family managed, and Lisa grew up with a relatively picture-perfect life—at least, it appeared that way on the surface. She had a home in the country with lots of land to explore and horses and dogs to play with. What more could a girl want? She was athletic, smart, compassionate, and kind to others. She seemed self-confident but perhaps a bit sad. Lisa's loneliness came from a place that no one knew about. Deep inside, she had secrets—several of which she did not even know about—and a sense of foreboding that loomed in her spirit even on her best days. Eventually, this feeling grew into depression as she ran out of things that she thought would bring her happiness. None of the conventional things brought her peace—not money, status, cars, or romance. Her achievements, her popularity, and even the deep love she had for her animals could not disperse the ugly feelings that lurked in her soul. Something inside her was just not right.

One day, Lisa's "cousin" asked her a simple question that would change everything. She was the daughter of her mother's best friend and someone who knew the family dynamics. They considered each other to be cousins because when you're adopted, anyone can be family. Anyhow, she asked Lisa, "Why do you hate yourself so much?" Well, the answer seemed obvious. Someone who had caused others pain from the time of conception, whose birth mother could not even look at her when she was born or even name her—how could she love herself? The people who had the most impact on her psyche sent a powerful message, and it was quite negative. Her adoptive family was not much comfort. When she had been abused and tried to communicate her pain, it was ignored. Lisa felt that she was not worth defending or even worth being heard. She thought of herself as trash; no one would care if someone broke her or even if she were thrown away. She felt unworthy and unloved, and she turned in on herself. Furthermore, in the house where she was raised, Lisa was told she was special—chosen even—but always seemed to be at fault for everything. She felt that she was the cause of everything that was wrong. So let me ask you, why in the world wouldn't Lisa feel contempt for herself? When parents don't act honorably and take responsibility for their own actions, their children carry their shame. When that shame is not talked about openly, it gets buried, and then it festers. Lisa wasn't just living with the monsters; now they were living inside her. According to her immature and judgmental mind, the case was closed! But this simple question that her cousin had asked resonated deep in her soul! Lisa knew somewhere inside that it was because of a secret wound that she was not yet ready to face, and it caused her to experience dissonance. Something just didn't mesh, and she could not close the door on it any longer!

All throughout her childhood, Lisa would retreat to a secluded place from time to time and think to herself that somewhere out in the world was her real mother—the person who would love her the way she should have been and needed to be loved. She often thought this was her birth mother, but instinct told her otherwise. Lisa also sensed her adoptive parents' trepidation about being usurped by Belle, so she did not desire to search for her. Lisa's brother, on the other hand, did search for and did find his birth mother. Unfortunately, his mother was unable to allow him into her life at first, and this reinforced the notion that Lisa should just let it go. The risks were not worth the reward, so she pursued a journey of self-discovery in other ways, which led her to realize that her perfect mother is God. Yes, I said God is not only her Father but her nurturing mother as well. Lisa developed a prayer life that steadily strengthened her faith and gave her the courage to face some of the truths about her past. As she read God's Word, she developed an increasingly intimate relationship with her heavenly mother/father/brother, Jesus. Her need to be accepted by the people around her all but vanished, and she no longer needed to be a people pleaser. When the Lord told her in secret the events that had caused her to hate herself, she began the process of forgiveness that started with herself. She had to learn how to love and forgive the worst enemy of all—the one in the mirror. Lisa found companions that allowed her to share her thoughts and feelings and eventually was able to go back to her adoptive family and continue the healing journey.

Around the time Lisa was twenty-three, her eldest brother, the oldest of the siblings in her adoptive family, was diagnosed with HIV. She was devastated because he was the only person with whom she felt safe. Twelve years later, when he had full-blown AIDS, he received hospice care. It was a somber time for the entire family—a time for reflection and for prayer. The hospice nurse, a wonderful and spiritual Black woman, spoke to Lisa one day. She told her that she needed to find her birth mother and put her at peace. Lisa had never thought about it like that. The fact that a reunion might benefit Belle made all the difference in the world. That her presence would not be an intrusion but a blessing was a new perspective. So the search began. It would be several years before the actual reunion would take place. Once the process was in full swing, there was no turning back.

The support group that Lisa attended helped tremendously as she prepared for the reunion. When Lisa did finally meet Belle, there was a flood of mixed emotions. It was like a secret portal had been opened, and for the first time in her life, she felt fully alive! *She had finally embraced the fact that she had two sets of parents—two parts to herself.* This realization is an underlying theme that you will see in the pages to follow, where this truth shows itself via a *dragonfly* as well as in the *ability to fly and defeat a menacing giant,* but more will be said about those things later. In addition to Belle, Lisa learned that she also had a sister who was several years younger than she was. The name that was on record as being Lisa's father was disclosed, but we'll call him Dan. He was also her sister's father, or so she thought. The first time Lisa talked to Belle on the phone, she learned that Dan was not her father; Belle had lied to social services. Lisa's father was a different man. Lisa's biological father was, let's just say, a date that went bad; Belle claimed that she had been raped.

Let me explain a little of the history here. Lisa's birth

grandmother had been orphaned as a child, and in her quest to find love (or whatever it was she was looking for), I was told that she accepted material favors from men. Like so many women of that generation, she brought her daughter, Belle, into that type of life. Perhaps that created a spiritual vacuum that set the stage for the darkness that would become Lisa's world. As the story went, on the night that Lisa was conceived, Belle had a tragic experience. It is unclear what really happened, but somewhere along the way, Lisa was told that her biological father was married and had two young children and wanted nothing to do with Belle—never mind an unintended child. Hearing this added one more thing to the list of things that caused Lisa to feel unloved and unworthy.

At the time Lisa was born, Belle had a dear friend, Dan, and when he learned of the pregnancy and the subsequent relinquishment, he married her, and the two attempted to get Lisa back from social services. They were ultimately denied, but Dan would still have an impact on Lisa's life. Because he was supportive, Belle married him and used his name instead of the name of the real father when she was giving nonidentifying information to the orphanage. Perhaps this was because the truth was too painful. During Lisa's search process, it was discovered that Dan had since died. He was not Lisa's father, but he was her half sister's father, and neither she nor Belle knew of his passing. They had lost touch because he had been caught in the act of adultery a few years after her half sister was born. Because of that, the couple divorced. Even though there had been no contact over the years, Lisa's sister had hoped to one day look him up. It was difficult for Lisa to carry the weight of knowing the truth of his death into their initial reunion, but it seemed to bring them all together a bit. What they had was an awkward bond, but it was a bond nonetheless. Getting to know her long-lost family was interesting. Thankfully, Lisa had waited to do it in God's timing, so she had minimal expectations, and her eyes were wide open.

In the beginning of the reunion, everything was new and exciting! They went to dinner, to Christmas activities, on a ferry ride to Provincetown, and on the Boston Duck Tours, and they gathered at each other's homes several times. Once, Belle even agreed to go to one of the adoption-triad support-group meetings. At the time of the reunion, Lisa was in her early forties and had been in a committed relationship with a wonderful and caring woman. What she never expected was that her partner felt threatened by the birth mother's reentry into Lisa's life. The dynamics of their relationship were shifting, and nothing seemed normal anymore. It was all surreal and difficult to process. It was especially difficult when Belle told her that she regretted not having an abortion. With so many new emotions and uncertainties, Lisa found the need for counseling. As luck would have it, one of the country's few adoption-issue specialists was based near where Lisa worked. With a bit of a fight from the insurance company, she received coverage to get the guidance that proved essential for her journey to wholeness. With the help of God, her therapist, the support group, and her loving partner, Lisa grew emotionally, and many of her oldest and deepest wounds were being healed.

As the reunion continued, it became blatantly obvious that dysfunction ran rampant in her birth family. As I mentioned before, Lisa's grandmother had been orphaned herself when the great-grandfather contributed to the death of the great-grandmother. The story goes that he had pushed his wife down a flight of stairs while in a drunken rage. The grandmother had been placed into foster care where she was subsequently violated. No one can be sure, but because of the "fruits of her life," one would suspect that she had been abused sexually. Of course, the darkness of it all spilled into her daughter's life: the life of Lisa's birth mother, Belle. I find it amazing that even with all that pain from the past, Belle was able to welcome Lisa with open arms at the beginning of their reunion. In the moment, it felt lovely. They both wanted desperately to feel connected and normal—like what Lisa perceived everyone else's life was like. Lisa didn't want to ruin the magic at first, but her partner's apprehension and several of Belle's comments threw up many red flags. One thing that was most troubling was that she was not allowed to spend time alone with her half sister. Belle insisted that she be present at all their gatherings. There were a lot of secrets that she did not want the two siblings to discuss, but some truths did surface. For instance, one day, when Belle had gone off to the bathroom, her half sister showed her pictures of another family and told Lisa that she had spent time in the foster-care system. Spending time with that other family might have given her what her own mother could not. Perhaps the experience helped her half sister to learn that someone else could give love and kindness. Perhaps it was what she needed, and it allowed a glimmer of light and healing into her life. Ultimately, it was beneficial for both. Lisa's half sister was able to bring some love back to her mother, Belle. Over the next two or so years, there were many other "forbidden" conversations, mostly phone calls between the sisters, and little by little, the big picture emerged.

Over time, the instincts of Lisa's partner would prove to be true. Lisa learned of Belle's true intentions after she was asked to be her health-care proxy. During the line of questions, Belle attempted to get her social-security number—something that is *not* needed on the health-care proxy forms. Thankfully, her half sister had tipped Lisa off by asking those very same questions the night before. The next day, when Lisa told Belle that her half sister had already asked all those questions, Belle replied, "That bitch."

There were other attempts to manipulate Lisa into doing things that were completely inappropriate. For instance, Belle tried to get Lisa to buy her summer cottage because she could no longer afford to keep it. She said that it would be an investment, but Lisa was not allowed to even so much as visit it. It seemed like it was all a scam so that Belle could hold on to the property. Obviously, Lisa declined the offer! Because of everything Lisa had already been through in her early life, she had learned to be persistent in "testing the spirits," and she had achieved a level of maturity that allowed her to see through all these schemes. Lisa was grounded and well connected to her higher power and able to navigate the chaotic maze that she found herself in.

Through the guidance of the Holy Spirit, Lisa was now able to step back and view the situation objectively. She could see things more clearly, and she was able to draw on Christ's strength to forgive these people who had hurt her—who had trespassed against her, as the Lord's Prayer says. After all, her birth mother didn't know any other way of life. Over a period of seven years, it became apparent that the relationship continued to be toxic and would likely never become truly healthy or beneficial to either party. Lisa deliberated long and hard, and with some help, she composed and delivered a compassionate Dear John letter to Belle. The reunion came to all but an end. Occasionally, cards were exchanged through the mail, but that was all that felt safe. It was sad in a way, but Lisa was joyful just the same to know the truth and to finally have her story. She could move on, knowing who her birth mother was. The funny thing is that what first drove Lisa to get help through therapy when she was an adolescent was the notion that her birth mother was a prostitute. It troubled her deeply, and she wondered, *If my mother was a prostitute, what does that make me?* Her counselor told her that if she could imagine that, why not imagine herself to be a princess instead? The problem was that either way, she was living in a world of fantasy. Now that she had journeyed to discover the truth—that she could be both the daughter of a harlot and a princess—she was free, and it felt amazing. Lisa had learned that two things can be true simultaneously. There was no more make-believe; she was ready to face life head-on.

Chapter 3

NOT MY NAME

LISA IS NOT my name, as I briefly explained in the previous chapter, but it is one of the names that God used to tell me who I really am. My name is not what is important because the focus here is on God's extraordinary abilities and the lengths to which She will go to heal us. Even in the darkest night of the soul and through the most horrific trials, love always wins! *Christ's name is what is important! To God be the glory!* Romans 14:11, referring to Isaiah 45:23, and Philippians 2:10–11 (NIV) tell us that *Jesus is the name that every knee shall bow to.* Because of what God did for us, *love always wins!*

Lisa is the part of me that I struggle to believe is real. It is the tormented part—my wounded inner child that is just emerging and needs to be made visible and be nurtured in ways that my adoptive parents were unable to provide. I have had many names. I was first named Carol by my foster family. I was given my legal name when I was adopted, and then during my reunion, my birth mother told me that she had secretly, in her heart, given me the name April because that was the month when I was born. The first card I ever received from her was for my birthday, and it was addressed to April. This presented yet another aspect of my identity that I needed to incorporate so that I could figure out who I am. All these emotions led me back to therapy. My first counseling session as a youth was with the local church minister. He lovingly told me to unlearn everything that I learned from the way I had been raised and to learn new coping methods. From there, I was referred to my first professional therapist, who was unable to deal directly with my intuitive knowledge. As I mentioned in the previous chapter, I had a nagging feeling that my birth mother was somehow involved in prostitution. I later learned that my instincts were indeed correct but also came to realize that even Jesus has Rahab, a prostitute, as part of His ancestral lineage. In Joshua 2, we learn that she married Salmon of the tribe of Judah and was the mother of Boaz, who fathered Obed, who fathered Jesse, who was King David's dad. The full lineage is found in Matthew 1:5. Needless to say, when that dude dismissed my feelings, I changed therapists and got the help I needed to get through that period of my life. I have always been guided by some force that was bigger than I am, and whenever I felt particularly alone or lost, I would find a feather in peculiar places. For years, I would just smile and think that the angels were looking out for me each time I found one. One day, to my astonishment, I realized that it was connected to Psalm 91:3–4 (ESV):

> For He will deliver you from the snare of the fowler and from the deadly pestilence. He will cover you with his pinions [feathers], and under his wings you will find refuge: his faithfulness is a shield and a buckler.

Wow! What a powerful message! The Creator of the universe guides me and protects me. Who needs parents anyhow? There are many scriptures that tell us that God will step in when our parents fail us.

Several years later, at the time of my reunion with my birth mother, I was referred to yet another therapist—one who specialized in adoption issues. From there, I was advised to see a hypnotherapist to help me get past my "overactive intellect" or tendencies to intellectualize because, as she said, that only served to build extremely defensive barriers for my mind to protect itself from painful realities. *During my very first hypnotherapy session, I was asked, "What did God name you?"* The therapist had no prior knowledge of me, so I knew this was God speaking to me through her. I knew from scripture that the very hairs on our heads are numbered (Luke 12:7). Let me back up a little and say that I had to petition the courts to release my original birth certificate, and because it had no name for me filled in, this question helped me to heal in so many ways. The hypnotherapist had no idea that I was having difficulty processing this no-name stuff. *When I had first seen my original birth record, it was like a punch in my heart. Seeing the document that I had fought so long and hard to get has no information about where my name should have been was devastating.* But there we were—the hypnotherapist doing God's work unknowingly. She told me she was stunned by the powerful force that she felt took over her when she asked me that question. What was also interesting was that when I had first arrived at the appointment, after some confusion about the address where we were meeting, she said that she had passed me on the road and thought that I was someone she knew—someone named Lisa. Wow, you cannot make this stuff up!

Here are a few fun facts that I found on the internet about the name Lisa. *Lisa* means "oath of God" or "pledged to God." *Lisa* means "female who is devoted to God." It is a female diminutive of *Elizabeth,* which comes from the Hebrew *Elisheba,* meaning either "oath of God" or "God is satisfaction." It is also a diminutive of *Bethia* (daughter or worshipper of God) and of *Bethany,* the name of a New Testament village near Jerusalem. Elizabeth was the mother of John the Baptist. My legal middle name is also a form of Elizabeth. Did God use the name Lisa because it was a code for discovering who I truly am? *To answer the question of what God named me, He named me Grace.* It just so happens that my legal name has Hebrew origins and means—wait for it—"grace"! So there I was with one blank birth record and one that had my legal first name and middle name. The legal document has hidden within those names Grace and Lisa—daughter of God!

THE STORY OF THE GIANT

As it turned out, having both birth certificates in my possession was a fulfillment of a reoccurring dream that I had as a child. When I was a young girl, I dreamed over and over again that a giant was terrifying the neighborhood. In that dream, if I held two pieces of paper, one in each hand, they gave me the power to fly. Because I was able to fly, I was able to defeat the giant, like David's stone that killed Goliath. Learning to fly gave me the ability to hit the giant right between the eyes, and then it was obliterated. I was like the very stone that David flung at Goliath.

Years later, when I had found my birth mother and petitioned the courts to release my original birth record, I came home devastated because, as I said earlier, it was blank. But here's the thing: as I went to put it away in my fire box, I had my legal birth certificate out as well. As I held them both, one in each of my hands, I had such a powerful epiphany! These were the two papers from my childhood dream—the very tools that gave me the power to fly. All along, with the dreams and the help of good people, God was leading me and helping me to remember that I am His precious child—one that He himself named before I was even conceived, just as it says in Psalm 27:10, Psalm 139:13–16, and Jeremiah 1:5. Here's the funny part: Because I was young, I really thought that I could actually fly, so I jumped off the front steps and landed hard, damaging both of my feet. I need to work on my landing! Throughout my childhood, I would wake up in agony because of foot and leg cramps. I would try to walk and just fall over. My dad would always get up and rub my feet until I fell back to sleep. So that you can visualize how this all affected me, I'd like to share this document with you. I will not share my legal birth certificate, which has my full name, but I have included a copy of my original one with the identifying sections blocked for privacy.

BROKEN AND BEAUTIFUL

Folks make jokes about someone being a crackpot, but I was not just cracked; I was a broken vessel. I can only explain how devastated I was after I saw that blank birth certificate by saying that it felt like I was a glass vase that had been totally shattered. There were broken pieces everywhere! You might ask how a person so emotionally damaged could be so strong and able to cope in such a positive manner. Ultimately, my faith was all I really had, and it was all I really needed. This truth gave me the freedom and the resilience I needed to get through my search and reunion and numerous other trials. Because others had failed me, I did not feel an obligation to please people and therefore was able to define myself according to my understanding of what God wants. After the reunion dust had settled, I thought I was all set and had been healed, but if I want to be completely *honest*, I had not fully recovered from my past. I realized that deep down, I was too guarded for my own good and still could not genuinely let anyone into my heart. I needed to finally admit to myself and to God that I did not yet trust Him completely. This lack of trust became a problem when I was taking on new leadership responsibilities at work. Life's pressures increased, and the cracks in my soul's foundation began to show themselves. For me to move on and realize my purpose, those cracks needed to be mended. I still had further to go in my faith walk. This is a journey that takes a lifetime. Unfortunately, many of us think there is some point of "arrival"—where we think that we've somehow made it. But then another storm hits—some unexpected setback or tragedy. Walking with God helps to anchor us and keeps us stable in spirit and gives us access to His power. Using these resources helps our "inner gardens" grow flowers of confidence, and when we do this, the giants in our lives do not stand a chance!

Chapter 4

NASCENCE

Nascence means "being born or coming into existence for the first time."

For you created my inmost being; you knit me together in my mother's womb.

—Psalm 139:15 (NIV)

LET'S GO BACK to where the story of "Lisa" began. It was the summer of 1985, and I was at a summer resort in the White Mountains of New Hampshire. I was one of the young women who had been hired to work and live there for the season. I was away from my family, and since I was not under the thumb of a boyfriend, I had a true level of independence for the very first time. Gaining some distance from what was familiar gave me a new perspective. Since I had not gone to a college away from home, this was my "college experience."

The other employees were all of college age, so this was a great opportunity for me to develop social skills. I did have some family ties to the establishment, so it wasn't completely foreign to me. These connections would prove helpful for what was about to unfold. The director of the camp had been there when my brother had been employed there a few years earlier, and the head of housekeeping was a friend of my parents and the former wife of a previous pastor at our family's church. Both people had some knowledge of my upbringing and were able to validate and guide me that summer.

Getting to the point where I was ready to venture out like that took some doing. The previous year, I was let go from my job because I had suffered such a debilitating depression that I could barely get out of bed. It took all my energy to make my way down the stairs to watch TV. Mind you, I only did that in the wee hours of the morning—between midnight and daybreak—and then I went back to the isolation of my bedroom. The company I had been working for was so gracious to me; they gave me chance after chance to get back on my feet, but to no avail. They ultimately needed to terminate my employment, and by that point, I was relieved not to have to keep trying to do what was at that point impossible. I needed to drop out of sight for a time and journey inside myself. The interesting part was that, perhaps for the first time in my life, I did not feel lonely. I sensed the spirit world more acutely.

Some spirits were terrifying, but I felt God's presence even more. Many months passed, and eventually, I was able to see a therapist. My mom's friend and one of her neighbors, who happened to attend our church, stopped by periodically while out on their daily walk and noticed my depressive state. They encouraged (or perhaps shamed) my mom to get me the help I needed. *I needed a resurrection to become something new—not just a reincarnation of a different version of the same old me.*

Just before I was hired to work in New Hampshire, I was getting "messages" from my grandmother—my adoptive mother's mom. I felt her presence but kept ignoring her. Finally, one day, I went back to my bedroom and saw that my "grandmother" doll mysteriously moved from my bookshelf to the floor across the room. I shrugged it off and put her back on the shelf, but then she ended up on the floor again the next day. This kept happening over and over. This doll was Mrs. Santa, who looked like a grandmother, and she was from the Annalee Gift Shop. She had been given to me by a friend of my parents when I was a child. Interestingly, the gift shop is located just down the street from the resort that I was about to be employed by. I believe it was my grandmother letting me know that she was there to help me in a way she never could while she was still living. I finally acknowledged her and thanked her for watching over me and encouraging me. I took the job, and from then on, my doll stayed on the shelf.

When I first arrived at the resort, it was intimidating. I was assigned a room along with a roommate. I was grateful that she was socially awkward like me—if not even more than I was. We were good for each other, and we grew so much that summer. Because of her shyness, I took the protector role. It pushed me to engage with the other employees more than I normally would have. I felt that I needed to be something of a big sister to her, and that responsibility was a blessing to me. We had many deep conversations as well as lighthearted laughs.

That summer, I met many new friends, and I kept in touch with a few of them for a few years afterward. I remember one staff party we had; it happened before the camp opened to the public, and it was a doozy! I was in awesome physical shape at that point and not ashamed to show it off a little; it helped my self-esteem. I wore a white tailored suit jacket with no shirt underneath it. I looked classy but daring, and it made me feel powerful. One of the young men told me I looked hot! He was a gentleman, so I took it as a compliment and did not feel threatened in any way. What a wonderful and liberating time it was for all of us! I remember that for some reason, there was sawdust on the floor that night, but I cannot remember why exactly. But what I do remember is that I lost the cross my mother had given me for graduation that night, and because of the sawdust, it was a hopeless cause to try and get it back. I was secretly glad to be rid of it because, like so many other gifts, it had come with strings attached. One of my new friends from that summer bought me a new one to replace it, and the whole exchange was so symbolic of being set free from a sense of obligation to my parents. I had so much fun; I enjoyed the hikes up the mountains, kayaked in the lake, and attended a nondenominational church on Church Island that one can only get to by boat. I was included on trips to the nearby general store, and of course, I loved the haunting sound of the loons at night. *The other girls in our dorm told me one day that they loved waking up to the scent of my cologne. At the time, I used a scent called Herbissimo (mountain juniper) because it was aromatherapy to me. The fact that they all liked it was so healing to my soul!* I was never so alive and was grateful for every minute I worked there.

> But thanks be to God, who in Christ always leads us in triumphal procession, and through us spreads the fragrance of the knowledge of him everywhere. (2 Corinthians 2:14 ESV)

One of the guests rented their cabin for the entire summer. They were on the "preferred guest" list, and I was assigned to care for them. They had two gorgeous Irish setters. The couple was a bit elderly and could not properly exercise the dogs, so when I went for my jogs, at their request, I took them with me. I felt as though I were driving a royal chariot with the two dogs running out in front of me with their long red hair flowing in the breeze! After experiencing so many wonderful things and having had enough social interactions and meaningful connections to feel grounded, "it" hit me like a ton of bricks!

It was late in the morning, and I had the day off. I was lying on my bed in my dormitory room and reading a book that my cousin had given to me; it was about how the Holy Spirit heals past hurts. Thinking that my pain came from being relinquished by my birth mother, I had no idea what was about to happen, so I read on with enthusiasm. After all, that problem was fixed when I was adopted, so I felt secure enough to read about hurts from the past with a lighthearted spirit. My intuition had told me not to read this while I was still living at my parents' home—and for good reason. *The story I found myself strangely drawn to was about a girl named Lisa.* The family dynamics in Lisa's story rang so true to me. I felt that the ghosts of my childhood were materializing at last, and I could relate to this girl in the story in a way that I had never known before. This story addressed the issues that I had long suffered in silence—issues that I had not dared to address. My soul was stirring as the plot was getting intense, but I could not stop reading. The story began by describing the dynamics of the parents' relationship and how they then related to Lisa.

By the end of the story, I dropped the book to the floor and lay there on my bed, feeling absolutely devastated. What had caused the dysfunction in Lisa's family was an event that took place when Lisa was an infant. The mother had walked in on the father taking advantage of the baby's sucking impulses. His penis was in the child's mouth. Then, to add insult to injury, Lisa's mother reacted very badly. Rather than protect her child, she grabbed her and threw her against the wall. Thinking that she was dependent on her husband, the mom was unable to see him as the problem. Her knee-jerk response caused her to react to Lisa as if she were "the other woman" rather than for what she really was—an innocent victim. Of course, Lisa could not remember the event; she was a baby when it happened, and the head injury probably had an amnesiac effect as well. I knew in my soul that this was what had happened to me as well. It may not have been exactly the same, but something very similar had taken place. All the dots were connecting for me; everything was suddenly very clear. Even with different details, the event would have had the same devastating effect on me and on my family. Now it was right in front of me—the demonic secret that had always been lurking in the shadows of my mind. My immediate response was to ask God, "Please do not let me know for certain if this is true or not until I am fully able to forgive lest I be led into the temptation to retaliate." Wow, that was a lot, but by God's grace, I got my bearings and left the quiet of the dorm room to hike to the top of my favorite mountain. I needed to feel closer to God.

DRAGONFLY

Later, when I felt a bit better, I came back down the mountain and attempted to go about my job as if nothing had happened. By this point in my life, I was good at this, so it was not impossible for me to compartmentalize my emotions. Thankfully, my next work assignment was to clean one of the smaller cabins and get it ready to receive guests. I was sent to do it alone, while the other girls went as a group to a larger cottage. In the safety of my solitude, my emotions began to surface, and I had never felt so overwhelmingly alone. The universe seemed to be an empty void and left me feeling that I had nothing to ground me. Without friends and with a family that I felt I could no longer draw any comfort from, I was numb, so I just stood there, not knowing where to turn, and breathed out a heavy sigh. Just then, a dragonfly flew into the cabin and startled me. My immediate reaction was to brush it away. Then I had an epiphany: This was one of God's creatures, and it was a connection to Him. I allowed it to rest on my chest—right over my heart—and I continued to clean. A while later, my new friend was still with me, and I was grateful for the companionship. I realized that the insect must have been growing weary or perhaps needed water or to flap its wings, so I stretched out a finger, and it hopped onto it. Then I brought the creature outdoors, and I thanked it for its kindness as it flew off and over the lake that was nearby. I thanked God for sending help and encouragement and knew that I would somehow survive this traumatizing truth.

THE LION AND THE LAMB

God always gives us what we need to gain victory over any circumstance. Psalm 46:1 (NLT) says, "God is our refuge and strength, an ever-present help in trouble." I found this to be true, even though I had just been dealt the most devastating blow of my life because I also had just made new friends. Perhaps because of this trauma, they would become real friends—ones I could share my true self with. They were two of the employees who worked with me that summer. Both had also suffered much throughout their childhoods, and the three of us drew strength from one another as we shared our faith in God. One day, the three of us went on a road trip together. As we were going along, lamenting the pain of our pasts, we were trying to play Madonna's "Love Don't Live Here Anymore" on the cassette player in my car. It was so strange; it would play the song just before it and the one just after it, but it would not play *that* song. We were growing frustrated with the machine because we all wanted to wallow in feeling sorry for ourselves. Just then, the three of us noticed simultaneously a large billboard along the road that read in big bold letters "Jesus Lives." We all agreed that love *does* live here still! How ironic and so fateful the timing was. If that weren't enough, there appeared in the sky a giant cloud that was so eerily and clearly in the shape of a lion with a lamb. None of us seemed to want to say anything to the others for fear that we were simply imagining it, but when I pointed it out, the others sighed a breath of relief and said that they too saw it and were stunned! The cloud then changed, and the lion and the lamb morphed into the shape of a white dragon, like the one in the movie *The NeverEnding Story*— the one that Atreyu rides to fight the Nothing. If you recall, the plotline of that movie is about a boy who leaves "reality" to get what he needs and then returns to give to his grieving father that which the father cannot give to him, the Water of Life. How strange that God would use this image in the clouds to comfort and inspire three wounded women. His plan is always perfect. You see, the utility van that was used at the resort that we all worked at was an old white VW van that was dubbed the White Dragon. That same van was the one that someone had jokingly attempted to run me over with just a few days prior. When they had gotten too close to me, they seemed to have hit an invisible wall. The van seemed to stop in its tracks, and the driver had such a puzzled look on his face, leaving me to smile to myself, knowing that it was the hand of God protecting me. The following year, I was promoted to assistant head of housekeeping, and the White Dragon was assigned to me! Those real-life experiences stayed with me in my memory for many years, reminding me to never give way to the *nothingness*—the despair that would frequently attempt to steal my joy, my hopes, and my dreams for the future.

I mentioned earlier that there were family ties to that summer resort where I worked in 1985. These ties helped to validate that the story was true—that there were indeed problems in the family that were not just in my imagination. These people at the resort knew my parents or knew of them enough to encourage me to break the cycle of self-defeating tendencies. The former pastor of the church that I was raised in had become the director of the camp when he retired from the ministry. This happened when he had reconnected with his own birth father, and divorcing his wife was part of his healing. I like to think that God sent him there ahead of me to set the stage for my healing before he remarried and moved on. His former wife ran the housekeeping department during the summer that I worked there. Without realizing it, the ex-wife's story intersected with my own, and she would occasionally say things that would assist me in seeing the big picture about my parents more clearly. My brother, who had once worked there, took a job at a nearby camp that summer, and I would ride my bike to see him on my days off. He also had some unfavorable experiences with my parents, and now that the two of us were out of our childhood home, we could talk freely and compare stories. That summer helped me bond with him and offered more insight. There were many other things that confirmed that God had indeed spoken to me and told me the truth through the story of Lisa. Slowly I was putting together the puzzle and was given the keys that would free me from the jail cell of denial and shame.

When I was relinquished, my birth mother had imagined that her child would be taken into a picture-perfect family and given a life of privilege—one free from troubles. She thought that giving up her baby would spare me the pain that had plagued and continued to plague her own life. She could not handle having a baby, and she wanted to give me a chance at a better life. She had a dream for her child that was unrealistic. No one's life is picture-perfect, and if it had been, I would never have gained the strength, wisdom, and fortitude necessary to be a blessing to others who have also suffered. Her intentions seemed right, but so did Peter's in the garden of Gethsemane. Sheltering a child from all harm can sometimes be like "helping" a butterfly to emerge from its cocoon or like helping an eaglet escape its egg. In both instances, the good intentions leave the creatures weak and unable to fly, so they die prematurely, never experiencing the lives they were meant to live.

Jesus tells us in John 16:33 (NIV) that in the world, you will have trouble, but you must take heart! He says, "I have overcome the world." This was the life path that I was on, and I was beginning to realize it. By allowing his children to suffer, God gives them both free will and independence. These trials can push a person into depression or send them into the center of the storm, where there is peace amid the chaos. This story is not the place to debate such profound truths in a general sense; it is enough to report what mindsets and beliefs helped me to achieve my personal victories. Romans 8:5 (NET) says, "For those who live according to the flesh have their outlook shaped by the things of the flesh, but those who live according to the Spirit have their outlook shaped by the things of the Spirit."

If I am asked from whence came my help, there is just one word: *Jesus.* He taught me what He meant when He said that we should "rejoice in our sufferings" (Romans 5:3–4 ESV). It produces character and confident hope. Even my faith is His gift. Ephesians 2:8–9 (ESV) says,

> For by grace you are saved through faith, and
> this is not from yourselves, it is the gift of God;
> it is not from works, so that no one can boast.

Grace is what pulled me, pushed me, comforted me, and guided me through each and every storm.

One of the most difficult trials I faced was overcoming a misunderstood application of the commandment that tells us to honor our mothers and fathers. Early on, when my cousin had first pointed out that my self-loathing was misguided, she also gave me a book: *Why Am I Afraid to Love?* by John Powell. In this book, I found a revelation that would have a profound effect on my ability to outgrow my childhood trauma. The book talks about self-image in chapter 3. It points out that when a parent demands respect and then does not act respectably, it creates resentment. When this resentment cannot be properly acknowledged (in this case, it is because the abuse could not even be remembered), it creates deep emotional conflict. How does one honor their mother and father when at the core of the relationship, their parents are not honorable? This relationship was a far cry from what my birth mother had hoped for, but God allowed it. How? Why? These questions were at the core of my distrust. Gaining a fuller understanding of the scriptures and why bad things are allowed to happen in this world was like slowly lifting the veil and a bit like a bride getting ready to kiss her new husband. Ezekiel 16 speaks of a baby being thrown out into a field and of God passing by and helping it to grow and then making a solemn oath and a marriage covenant. It is speaking about Jerusalem being an adulterous wife, but the lesson applies to us all. I rediscovered this same book years later. It was on the bookshelf of a woman who would aid in bringing about another real turning point in my life.

MY REAL-LIFE FRIEND LISA

It was late at night, and the two of us had just met at a nightclub earlier that evening. There was an expectation that we were going to the apartment for sex, but instead, this woman wanted to get to know me. I was in a state of confusion; I wanted to let someone get to know me, but I had so many painful secrets, and there was so much to risk. As I paced the floor, trying to decide whether to stay or to go, I noticed the book and took it from the shelf. I opened it to the very same pages that I had read way back when I first began to wonder why I hated myself. Was this a coincidence or was the Holy Spirit guiding me? I did stay that night. We talked, and the two of us became soul sisters. We shared our painful stories with each other, and eventually, this new ally became my roommate, or should I say, I became hers. Eventually, we moved to another apartment, and then after a few years, she moved into my parents' house—my childhood home—with me, but just for a season. We were waiting for renters to move out of my deceased grandparents' house, so we stayed with my parents for the summer. My friend started to complain about the things that I had been silent about for years; she was afraid that I was not seeing things clearly. She saw for herself the family dynamics, validating what I could never have proven. This was a *huge* encouragement to me.

SOUR AND SWEET

Not every memory was bad. Looking through the lens of my dear friend helped me to name my issues and therefore move them to the periphery rather than the subconscious. This cleared my mind so that I could now at least notice some of the more pleasant memories. There were many things in my early years that were wonderful. Here are a few: There were midnight tea parties with Mom when I couldn't sleep, and sometimes we would have Nabisco Royal Lunch crackers in milk. My mother loved to knit and made me many beautiful sweaters; each one was one of a kind. When it came time for back-to-school shopping, I was allowed to pick out nice clothes—things that I really enjoyed wearing. On grocery-shopping day, we would go to the lunch counter in the market, and I would enjoy my most coveted treat—chocolate pudding in a sundae cup with whipped cream. Christmas was my favorite, especially Christmas Eve—when my family and our relatives all gathered at my aunt and uncle's house; he was the uncle who had built our house. My cousins and I could play, and Santa always made an appearance. There would be the sound of jingling bells, and footsteps could be heard on the roof, and the children would all glow with excitement as we anticipated his arrival! More than this, though, I loved the 11:00 p.m. candlelight service at church that just our immediate family would go to after the festivities and gift-giving. It was in these quiet moments that I felt most at peace. There were many happy events, but somehow, back then, they were always clouded by a deep sense that something was wrong, and I felt guilty for it. I felt as if I were somehow ungrateful. Eventually, I would learn that much of life is not either/or and that two things could be true simultaneously. It's "tastier" that way—like sweet *and* sour chicken. I learned that I could be both appreciative of the blessings in my life and, at the same time, be angry and hurt by some of those very same things.

MIDNIGHT AND LITTLE JOHN

The *most* impactful and major joy-inducing experience—one that offset much of the negativity—happened when I was about seven years old. My siblings and I were allowed to have a horse. He was all black, and his name was Midnight. I loved him then and still see him occasionally in my dreams. The horse was a blessing, and we all shared the responsibility of having him. They were old enough to have real jobs, so I had to get a paper route to help to pay for the horse's food and care. At first, we boarded Midnight at our relatives' place as they had a property that was fully equipped to care for the animal. They had a large barn with ponies and a donkey named Alex. Later, after we had built a barn on our own property, a wild pony from my uncle was given to me to train since I was the only one who had dared to ride it. His name was Little John, a brown Shetland pony with a white mane. Having these responsibilities was good for my development. The horses provided equestrian therapy. I could write an entire book about my horse and my pony. They were my friends, they understood me, and they gave me a sense of being grounded and more confidence than any human could. They helped me to learn to trust.

BLINDED SO THAT I COULD SEE

When I was a teen, my family was visiting friends in New Hampshire. They had a weekend cabin in the mountains, and it was near a lake. It was one of my favorite places to go. I was frequently permitted to bring my "cousin" along with us, and these times are a part of her treasured memories as well. Having friends along was a big deal because we didn't have them overnight to our own house very often. There was one weekend when my eldest brother was with us, and he had brought along his roommate. It was late in the season and a bit chilly, but I still wanted to go waterskiing. My "uncle" was an adventurer like me, so he said yes. He had taught me how to ski on one ski, and I was pretty good at it. Because of the cold, I took off from a seated position on the dock rather than from in the water so that I could stay dry and a little warmer. It went off without a hitch, and I was having a ball! My father, my brother, and his friend were all watching from the dock. When it was time for me to stop, I attempted to do what I usually did with two skis on, and that was to glide in and sit back on the dock without getting wet. This time was different—*very* different! As I approached the dock, I saw angels. I don't know how many there were, but it seemed like hundreds of them were all around me. The next thing I knew, I was coming to, and the men were all soaking wet. I had miscalculated, and rather than gracefully gliding into my landing, I hit the dock with my head. The impact was so forceful that it separated the raft end that was held on by large pins and sent the men into the water. They took me to the hospital, and then, with my eyes wide open, everything went black. It was terrifying to lose my vision! I kept saying, "I can't see, I can't see!" The doctor told me that it was possible that my retinas had detached, but now I believe that my blindness was caused by my brain swelling. By some miracle, my sight did come back, but this did not happen until I understood *clearly* what God was telling me. He told me not to trust what I could see with my eyes but to trust Him to show me what is true. A few years later, on the way to a prayer meeting, I was telling that story to a friend of mine. She was an older woman whom I had met at work, and I think that God put it on her heart to help me. She had picked me up at my house, and I remember that for some reason, I did not have any other form of transportation at the time. Anyhow, she said to me that sometimes, a head trauma like that can reverse the effects of an earlier amnesic event. I had no idea what she was talking about at the time, but as I look back, it was most definitely, absolutely God waking me up! What the devil tried to do to harm me by using my mom to throw me against the wall, God reversed to use for His glory! Praise Jesus!

FATHER, FORGIVE THEM. THEY KNOW NOT WHAT THEY DO

My first response and my continued prayer throughout the years was that God *not* let me know for certain if all of this was true—not until I was fully able to forgive. Some twenty-eight years later, at my father's deathbed, the truth burst forth in a dramatic way. Let me back up a minute here. As you can imagine, I had first protested having to care for my parents. I loved them and I hated them all at the same time. I just wanted to keep my distance and live my own life. How could God ask me to do this? It just seemed cruel and demoralizing that I should have to become so intimate with the very people who had all but destroyed my sense of self-worth—even my will to live. What I wanted, and my sense of justice were overridden by the fact, and that I knew enough to realize that God knows best. My parents protested my care at first, but in the end, the experience brought out the secrets, and the truth blessed us all. I went from having a victim's mentality to becoming a victor. I learned to defeat my demons and love my enemies as well as myself.

I should explain that on the day before Dad died, two of the hospice workers were in my father's room. Somehow the subject of keeping family issues swept under the rug came up. We discussed how times were different back then and that a couple who had been scrutinized by social services during the adoption process would be more likely to keep silent about certain issues for fear that the family would be broken apart and that an incident with one child might cause the other children to be taken away. My father was unable to speak at this point, but his body went into some sort of convulsion.

The hospice workers said, "He heard that!" As the hospice team went about their business, I sat next to his bed, held his hand, and whispered, "It's OK, Dad. I know. God told me a long time ago, and I forgive you." He immediately relaxed. Years earlier, he broke down and sobbed; he said, "You'll never forgive me. You'll never forgive me." I had no idea at the time what he needed forgiveness for but assured him that I did and that he just needed to forgive himself. Now I knew what he had been crying about all those years ago. Later that day, one of the girls who worked in the nursing home came into the room while ranting about a child-abuse story that she had just heard—one about a man who hurt a baby. It seemed that she was sharing this for no apparent reason, but the Holy Spirit had set it up, and again my father's body responded to her words. This time, it was my life partner—the one person who would most likely want to retaliate for what he had done to his daughter—who was able to whisper words of grace and forgiveness to him. Meanwhile, I was able to address the issue of child abuse with the worker, confirming my own resolve to live in forgiveness. This allowed my father to hear how I truly felt, and I took advantage of the opportunity to offer a different response to a problem that affects so many people. By God's grace and wisdom and with my partner's assistance, I was able to address the needs of everyone in the room. My father died in peace the very next day.

MOM'S BEST GIFT EVER

My mother and I had a similar exchange just a few weeks earlier. She passed away just forty days prior to my dad's death. My parents' neighbor at the house where we grew up had said that she was quite surprised that Mom died before Dad. I did not think all that much of it at the time, but in the years that followed, I realized how much it took for her to relinquish that control. One time, I had been talking with a minister who was also a licensed psychiatrist, and my dad had agreed to go with me to talk things out. Secretly, my hope was to absolve my father while he still had life in him to enjoy the freedom of losing his guilty conscience. When my mother caught wind of it, she put a quick end to that notion, and my father never defied her. So, in the end, her greatest gift to herself, to my dad, and to all of us was simply getting out of the way and letting me have those last forty days with my dad.

Before she died, we were alone together in her room at the assisted-living facility. Dad was in the nursing home that was just across the parking lot. She was thirsty, so I got her something to drink. As I gave it to her, I said once again that I loved her, and rather than say "So what?" which she had been saying to me during her last days, this time, she struggled to say the words "I love you too." She had a look in her eyes that told me that she understood that the love I spoke of was by the grace that only Christ can give. I loved her *not* because of anything she ever gave me, and I loved her despite how she had failed me. Finally, she could say, in *all* sincerity, that she loved me. Those were the last words my mother ever spoke. My mother died in peace just a few days later. My persistence to overcome paid off. By God's grace, I had brought to both of my parents the Water of Life, like Bastian was able to in *The NeverEnding Story*.

DOLPHINS

A few days later, my prayers for assurance were answered by two powerful confirmations that my parents were now in paradise. One was a report that my brother, who was on a cruise at the time of Dad's passing, had—that very morning—seen two dolphins frolicking in the wake and reported back to his partner that he had just seen Mom and Dad. He had no idea at the time that Dad had *just* died. The other was a report from "my cousin" that Dad's spirit had visited her that same night, and he looked so happy and healthy and seemed to be around fortyish—the age he was when they adopted me. I sobbed when she shared that with me. Those stories' details are for another time, but knowing that they were with Jesus, I knew that I was finally, truly able to forgive—nearly thirty years after God first spoke my truth to me. Reflecting on my journey and assessing the past before going forward into what promised to be the best years of my life, I pondered what I would say if I were asked the question, "Is adoption a good thing?" My answer would be to say, "It depends on how you define *good*. No one gets through life without problems. It's just the world we live in, and all we can control is how we choose to respond." I chose to live by the example of the dolphins and frolic in the wake.

FIRST EXPERIENCE AND MY DYING WISH

I was just five years old when I lost the first person in my immediate family. We were at my paternal grandfather's funeral, and I knew right there and then what I wanted to be when I grew up—I wanted to be dead. My subconscious death wish was surfacing, but what I really wanted was that peace that the minister spoke so eloquently about. What I came to realize was that the peace that surpasses all understanding (Philippians 4:7 ESV) is only found when you die to self and your ego. It's putting God first, wanting and doing His will rather than your own. John 8:32 (NLT) tells us, "And you will know the truth, and the truth will set you free." It is the truth that sets us free and allows us to rise from the ashes of dysfunction like a phoenix! Romans 8:15 (ESV) says, "For you did not receive the spirit of slavery leading again to fear, but you received the Spirit of adoption, by whom we cry, 'Abba, Father.'"

God *is* my father and my king. In William Shakespeare's play *Henry VIII*, the king says in reference to his daughter:

> Nor shall this peace sleep with her; but as when
> The bird of wonder dies, the maiden Phoenix,
> Her ashes new create another heir
> As great in admiration as herself;
> So shall she leave her blessedness to one,
> When heaven shall call her from this cloud of darkness,
> Who from the sacred ashes of her honour
> Shall star-like rise as great in fame as she was,
> And so stand fix'd.

A crown of beauty instead of ashes. (Isaiah 61:3 NIV)

Chapter 5

MY FATHER'S BUSINESS

> And he said unto them, "Why
> were you looking for me?
> Did you not know that I must be
> about my father's business?"
>
> —Luke 2:49 (NKJV)

THE PREVIOUS CHAPTER was named "Nascence" because it means "being born or coming into existence for the first time. The nascence of a business idea is very exciting for an entrepreneur. The noun nascence is commonly used to talk about the development of something new or the emerging of great potential" (Vocabulary.com). *Potential*—now that's a powerful word. We are all born with great potential, but so few ever reach it. Maslow calls this self-actualization in his hierarchy of needs.[1] The world sometimes seems to be set up

---

[1] Abraham H. Maslow, "A Theory of Human Motivation," *Psychological Review* 50, no. 4 (1943): 370–396, https://doi.org/10.1037/h0054346.

as one big obstacle course, challenging many of us to just give in and give up. Far too often, there seems to be a shortage of mentors and encouragers to keep us on the straight path that leads to real success. We can't even agree on what success is. How many times do we see a supposedly successful person take their own life or OD on drugs or alcohol?

But there is hope! The world is now connected in unprecedented ways and is changing in ways that we never could have imagined. Not all these changes seem good or at least not at first. Anything that is unfamiliar often seems a little scary. But have faith; God is still large and in charge. I believe that we are moving toward a promised time. Similar to the Old Testament's promised land, we are entering into a time that is a culmination of all that has been and a vision of how life is meant to be—not just for the fortunate few but for every single soul that exists. But this won't happen all on its own. Each person needs to embrace their own unique potential.

At the time of this writing, I had recently left a nineteen-year career because the company I was working for no longer matched my values. We were growing in different directions, so it was time to part ways. The business opportunity that I had spent months investigating and negotiating with to come on board fell apart three weeks after I started my new job. As tempted as I was to feel pity for myself, fall into despair, and settle for working for anyone who would hire me, I couldn't help but believe that this was my opportunity to reinvent myself. Maybe I could turn the page and have a second act that was worth talking about and could run my race and have a fabulous finish! I have never been one who enjoys attention, but it doesn't scare me either—at least not anymore. As my faith has grown, so has my self-esteem. I have a courage that comes from knowing *whose* I am rather than just who I am. I know that God loves me so much that He sent His Son to die for me. This might sound a little narcissistic, but I feel that I am special—but no more so than you. What if I could make it my business to help people, businesses, and governments become what they were meant to be? I realize that I cannot change the world. I don't have that kind of control, nor would I want it. Besides, I would most certainly mess things up, but I can let God change *me*. As Plutarch said, "What we achieve inwardly will change outer reality." Mother Teresa put it this way: "I alone cannot change the world, but I can cast a stone across the water to create many ripples."

We all have so many gifts and talents that are just waiting to be tapped into. It's like a huge treasure chest of human resources that just needs to be unlocked. Together, we can have the lives we dream of. The dream looks different to each and every individual, but there are some commonalities that link us together as a global society. Differences are beautiful and need to be embraced, not feared. I have found that when people are secure with themselves, they do not reject those who are unique or different from the "usual suspects" in their lives. I believe that as children, we are naturally curious about people who are different, but somewhere along the way, we are taught to fear. Sometimes these messages are spoken, but most commonly, we learn them by the examples others set for us. This is similar to the way that most of us are taught to fear the dark—something many people live with without realizing it. So why do we continue to create "us and them" scenarios when it comes to community living? The scriptures tell us that all things work together for those who love God (Romans 8:28 NLT), but therein lies the problem as well as an opportunity. There are so many people who either don't love God or have no idea who God really is. Most of us think that we know and either accept or reject religion. Then we fight over whose religion is the right one. But what if every one of us was wrong? What if *no one* knew God? I mean, seriously, how could we? He is infinite, and we are so small. Even the physical and spiritual giants are puny to him, and in the stories we are all fed, these are usually men. Mind you, *He* is just a pronoun. Rather than embrace and submit to and be transformed by the divine Creator, historically, *men* have created a god in their own image and shoved their arrogant views and beliefs down everyone's throats. *I believe there is a "Lisa" in all of us.* I seriously doubt that the Creator of the universe is limited to one gender or the other. What if we could be secure enough to be OK with not knowing? What if we allow ourselves and others to embrace the idea that the Creator is so far beyond what we could possibly comprehend? What if we accept that mystery and uniqueness within ourselves and encourage it in everyone we encounter? What if?

ESCAPING BOXES

When I was just seven years old, my family thought I was nuts. There is some truth to that, but it depends on who is defining *sanity*. One day, I gathered them all around me to show them a diagram that I had drawn of a whole bunch of little three-dimensional boxes. I explained that in our minds, we are all in little boxes, and then I proceeded to tell them that I was going to find a way to get out of mine. Then, once I was free, I would help everyone else get out of their box. It has taken me another fifty-plus years, but I am proud to say that I am free and without my box—mostly, LOL! Staying out of it can be a daily challenge. The scriptures describe this phenomenon in Galatians 5:1 (NIV): "It is for freedom that Christ has set us free. Stand firm, then, and do not let yourselves be burdened again by a yoke of slavery," while verses 4 to 6 warn us not to fall away from grace.

Because of the recurring dream that I spoke of earlier—the one where if I held two pieces of paper, one in each hand, I would have the power to fly—I had realized that I was always meant to find out who I really am. I was not going to be satisfied with just what people had told me but would dig deep, be tenacious, strengthen my resilience, and never ever give up! As an adult, I realized the symbolic significance of the five stones that David had gathered when he went against the enemy in the name of God. Five is the number for grace—God's grace. Even though I felt lost, unwanted, unworthy, and abandoned as a child and throughout most of my adult life, I can see now that *God has always been with me, guiding me and grooming me to be about His business*. I feel that He is grooming you too. If you look deep into your heart, you will know that I'm telling the truth. If you need more proof, remember what Jesus told the disciples back then and is still telling us now: "The harvest is plentiful but the workers are few. Ask the Lord of the harvest, therefore, to send out workers into his harvest field" (Matthew 9:37–38 NIV). In Luke 10:2–3 (NIV), He adds, "Go! I am sending you out like lambs among wolves." Galatians 6:9 (NIV) encourages us; it says, "Let us not become weary in doing good, for at the proper time we will reap a harvest if we do not give up."

KILLING CORPORATE

Giving up and giving in to despair are *huge* temptations to me and probably many of you. After leaving my nineteen-year career, as I said, I lost my next job just three weeks later. It took a long time to see the blessing in all that had happened—partially because I was avoiding the truth of how I had played a role in those events. Everyone, including that place of employment, said that my having been let go was not my fault, and it wasn't, but that did *not* mean that there wasn't a great lesson to be learned from all of it. A few months later, I was recruited for a management position in an industry about which I had no job knowledge. I was willing to learn, and they were willing to teach me. I was so excited to finally have what I thought was the perfect career for me! The commute, salary, and benefits package were all exactly what I had been praying for. Two months later, the CEO showed up at the office and sat down with my manager and me to tell me that I was not the right fit for that position. Once again, they affirmed that I had not done anything wrong. I was given all the money that I had earned, one free month of health insurance, and extra pay that was equal to two weeks of my salary. Obviously, I was not being fired. We talked for some length as to how they wanted to make sure that I did not get into a negative mindset about the loss of yet another job, and I agreed. I would encourage myself and share my insecurities with God and with my partner, but how could I not be tempted to think that this would just keep happening? *I struggled to keep from feeling worthless, and I just wanted to crawl into a cave and never look for work again.* I was not to blame, but there *had* to be some lesson in all of this! Sometime later, I learned from a former coworker that I "didn't fit" because I was not codependent like the regional manager or the owner of that business. The truth was that one of the men that I supervised had called in the night before, threatening to give his resignation. He was drunk when he called. The day before, he had assaulted me verbally and was infuriated when I kept my cool and handled things professionally. The encounter was so bad that a customer who had witnessed it called the store to offer me encouragement. That employee was confronted by another worker who was there; she laid into him how inappropriately he had spoken to me, and then he asked me how I was doing. Ultimately, my boss chose to keep him and let me go. A few months later, they had to fire him because, as I was told, he came to work intoxicated. I'm not happy about any of that, but I must admit that I do feel vindicated.

Coincidently, at that time, I was reading Sue Monk Kidd's book *The Dance of the Dissident Daughter.* My book-club friends had chosen it, and we all enjoyed the profound truths we were finding within its pages. What eventually occurred to me was that my real life was playing out in a similar way to the author's own story of awakening. I came to realize that all three of my jobs had one commonality: They all supported the institution of patriarchy but in a variety of ways. My nineteen-year career was steeped in the old-boy-network mentality despite their attempts to be progressive. At that job, I was told, "Perhaps you just don't fit the corporate mold." No shit, Sherlock! God literally told me to leave that job. Then that business was devastated when COVID-19 hit, and again, I was not happy but vindicated. My next job was a prime example of what the book describes as female bullishness (p. 246). The author was describing a woman she met at a retreat who claimed to be "a strong woman like her mother." She goes on to say, "Eventually the woman recognized that like the rest of us, she and her mother had their own wounded feminine life inside, that they too, had been severed from their feminine souls and because of that had learned to mimic the ways of patriarchy. What they mistook for female strength and authority was recycled patriarchal power." My coworker at that job had explained to me one day that she had only gotten to where she was in life because of her abrasiveness. She called it something different, but her attitude felt like sandpaper to me. I considered being around her to be an opportunity to smooth out my rough places—to see myself reflected in her and adjust accordingly. In one of our conversations, I shared with her that I understood what she meant and that I agreed that sometimes we needed to be tough to get to where we were, but I also told her that I had come to realize that to get to where I want to go, I need to readjust and become gentler. Any true leader will attest that there is power in being vulnerable. At my third job, the issue arose in the form of fear of confrontation, which was demonstrated by my manager. In his attempts to "keep the peace," he was actually creating a disingenuous and dysfunctional environment. It is interesting how these things can creep into your life in such clever disguises. So many ways to misuse or fail to use our God-given authority!

What, then, should power look like? It should be the kind that God approves—where it glorifies the Creator, honors ourselves, and serves our neighbor. Unfortunately, we don't have an abundance of role models for that kind of power. Thankfully, we do have one: grace. Describing the power of God, or even Jesus, is subject to interpretation and bias, but *grace is grace! Grace builds up where others would tear it down. Grace heals where others would wound. Grace is resilient when others would give up. Grace is the Spirit that Jesus promised to send us when He ascended into heaven. Grace is the power to overcome evil with goodness.* Sue Monk Kidd describes *authentic power* as "not ruthless, controlling, self-serving, dominion-seeking ... it is *not* staying up by keeping others down ... it is potent, forceful power, yes, but one that is also compassionate, that enables others as well." On page 231, she quotes Carolyn Heilbrun, who said, "Power is the ability to take one's place in whatever discourse is essential to action and the right to have one's part matter."

I believe that real power is the ability to be vulnerable and indomitable simultaneously. Wait—what? How in the world could anyone pull *that* off? The thing is, no one can—not with their own strength anyway, and that's the perfect plan of God. I have a devotional that was written by Sarah Young. It is titled *Jesus Calling*. It is written in the first person—as if Jesus himself is speaking directly to you. On the page written for September 2, it reads, "You accept weakness as a gift from Me, knowing that My Power plugs in most readily to consecrated weakness." The apostle Paul speaks a lot about this concept in many of his writings. For me, I see it as *God in me and me in Him!* I too am about the Father's business! Amen and amen.

Chapter 6

212 / 12:12

WATER BOILS AT 212 degrees; it turns into steam and is powerful enough to move a locomotive. When God turns up the heat, so to speak, it's not to punish us so much as it is to strengthen and purify us. When anger is handled in a righteous way, it fuels us to do things that fear would normally hold us back from. "When bad things happen to good people" and to bad people too, it quite often is a matter of perspective that makes us see these things that happen to us as bad. So often in life, when we look back, it is those very events that shape us. We can allow our troubles to mold us for the better or the worse because we have been given free will. We have the freedom to choose how we will respond to life's circumstances. Far too often, people think that when things go "wrong," we must have done something to deserve the misfortune. Sometimes our hardships are the result of poor choices, but even then, God gives us even more grace. Our

Creator waits patiently and yearns for us to return, and it's often in our time of trial that our bonds of intimacy are forged.

YOU CHOOSE: POSTTRAUMATIC STRESS OR POSTTRAUMATIC GROWTH

> Therefore, since we have been justified by faith, we have peace with God through our Lord Jesus Christ. Through him we have also obtained access by faith into this grace in which we stand, and we rejoice in hope of the glory of God. Not only that, but we rejoice in our sufferings, knowing that suffering produces endurance and endurance produces character and character produces hope, and hope does not put us to shame, because God's love has been poured into our hearts through the Holy Spirit who has been given to us. (Romans 5:1–5 ESV)

Wow! So how do we process all of that? When I first read this scripture passage, I thought, *What kind of sadistic mentality came up with this idea?* Why in the world would I ever welcome trials and hardships? In subsequent readings of these verses, the word *shame* stood out to me. Shame is a destructive emotion; it blocks us from using our gifts and talents. It tells us to hide our light and withdraw. Some guilt and remorse can be good, and without them, we might all become sociopaths, but shame is different. How often do we carry the shame of what was done to us as if we should perpetually pay for the sins that have been passed on to us? The children of divorced parents often blame themselves. Some parents even tell their children or imply in some way that they are to blame. Perhaps this self-blame is a coping mechanism that helps them feel in control in some strange way. When we blame ourselves, we have the illusion that if we change *our* behavior, we can change our environment. Otherwise, we might risk total despair and hopelessness. This only happens because we have not yet learned to trust God. *Children who have suffered sexual abuse most definitely blame themselves. I can tell you that every single time I hear the words "Your sins are forgiven," I struggle with my self-esteem because I still find it difficult to distinguish between my own sins and those of the people who have hurt me and who could not or would not take responsibility for it!* It's not for me to judge, and God does a much better job in addressing these issues as his goal is always to be redemptive and not so focused on the punitive aspect of correction. I can say that as a child, my only desire was to leave this world and go to heaven. I realize now that the wish was based on escapism because now that my parents have died, I am not in such a hurry to get there, knowing that I will see them again. I have much work to do!

BUBBLES ON JUDGMENT DAY

So how will Jesus "separate the lambs from the goats," and how do we discern the right path forward? Let us remember the full text of Matthew 25. The goats are those who did not help; they focused only on themselves and ignored the least among us. They may follow all the rules but miss the spirit of the law. The lambs dare to love even the "unlovable" and are not afraid to break the laws that man has created—laws usually used as a measure of being prideful and often formed out of arrogance and fear of vulnerability. Salvation requires confession, but when and to whom is confession safe and appropriate? How do we forgive our most heinous enemies— the ones in our own family? Only God can see clearly into our hearts. Even we can deceive ourselves, so we must learn to trust the process and allow Him to walk us through this wild maze called life. Unconfessed sins, whether they be known or not, of our own making or those done to us will fester and become toxic. There are many ways that we use to suppress pain: distraction, substance abuse, compulsiveness—you name it. So how can we ever confess that which we are not conscious of? Keep in mind that confession is not only an admission of guilt; it is also simply getting things off your chest. *When we learn to trust God, we can allow our feelings to bubble up.* When they are up on the surface, we can deal with them appropriately, but when we stuff them, they deceive us. For example, I have always suppressed my anger, and because of that, I did not realize that my anger was a mask for more vulnerable feelings—sadness and hurt.

After high school, I attended beauty school. I wasn't sure why; I just knew that it was something I needed to do. As it turns out, my birth mother was a hairdresser, and I believe that my gut and the Holy Spirit were leading me to find her and to find myself. Hairdressing was not my cup of tea because it all seemed so superficial to me. When you feel terrible about yourself, it doesn't matter how beautiful your hair is. I switched courses and went into esthetics instead. I was drawn to the concept more than anything because it taught everyone taking that course to bring the impurities of the skin to the surface and clean them away and then enhance that pure beauty with cosmetics when appropriate. Steam (the water that boils at 212 degrees) is used to open the pores, promote circulation, release acne-causing bacteria, release trapped sebum, and hydrate the skin. I liked the idea of exposing my inner beauty and was excited to learn how to sparkle and shine! I completed the course and was licensed as an esthetician but never practiced my craft, or so I thought. I realize now that I am a spiritual esthetician and have been fine-tuning my chosen profession in everything I do. I find it interesting that the difference between an esthetician and an aesthetician is one of specifics or generality. The former specializes in the beautification of the skin, and the latter is "a person who is knowledgeable about the nature and appreciation of beauty, especially in art." One little letter brings us from skin-deep to universal acknowledgment of all that is lovely. Even a scripture reminds us to look for that which is lovely: Philippians 4:8 (NIV): "Finally, brothers, whatever is true, whatever is honorable, whatever is just, whatever is pure, whatever is lovely, whatever is commendable, if there is any excellence, if there is anything worthy of praise, think about these things." It's true that "garbage in equals garbage out." Be mindful of what seeds you plant in your head if you want to reap a healthy harvest. We are what we eat, and just like food for the body, it's important that we watch the things that we feed the mind and the spirit.

As I was contemplating whether to write this book, the words *bubble up* kept showing up. In my morning devotional on November 9 in the book *Jesus Calling*, it tells its reader, "Sit quietly with Me, letting all your worries bubble up to the surface of your consciousness." Later that day, I attended an evening service where the minister's sermon was about the foot of the cross—where we find Jesus, who suffers with us—and that we need to let things bubble up. Then, when I went to get my taxes done, a form was never mailed to me, so I needed to call my previous employer. I got a callback from corporate that said that they were investigating the issue and that "it was all bubbling up." Hmm, interesting!

It fascinates me that water comes to a boil at 212 degrees (not 210 or 220) and how often the number twelve is used in scriptures. Here are just a few of the examples: Romans 12:12 (ESV) tells us to "rejoice in hope, be patient in tribulation, be constant in prayer." Genesis, particularly Genesis 35:22 and Genesis 49:28, tells us of the twelve tribes. In the New Testament, we learn about the twelve disciples, which are mentioned specifically in Matthew 10:1 and Mark 3:14. In Matthew 14:13–21, Mark 6:31–44, Luke 9:12–17, and John 6:1–14, we find the story of the twelve baskets full of leftovers after Jesus fed multitudes for the first time. In Matthew 15:32–39 and Mark 8:1–9, He does it again, but this time, it was for the Gentiles rather than the Jews, and there were only seven baskets full of leftovers, but the significance of that is a story for another day. There are twelve minor prophets in the Bible, and there are twelve stars surrounding Mary and the woman of the Apocalypse in Revelation 12. There are twelve imams in Islam. There are twelve hours in the day and twelve in the night, and there are twelve months in a year. Twelve makes a dozen, and even AA uses a twelve-step program for recovery. Hebrews 12 is our Creator's call to respond gratefully and nobly to the great invitation, reminding and inspiring us to not grow weary. As

Dory would say in *Finding Nemo*, "Keep on swimming, keep on swimming." The story of Veronica is a tale of persistence. She was the woman in the pages of Matthew 5, Mark 5, and Luke 8 with the bleeding issue who was cured when she finally got to see Jesus and touch the hem of his clothes. By the way, she bled for twelve years, and Jesus healed her on his way to resurrect the twelve-year-old girl who had just died.

I don't particularly put a lot of stock in angels, but I am open-minded. I kept seeing 12:12 on the clock, and it caused me to wonder. It is reportedly the mirror hour. According to willowsoul.com, seeing this number can mean the following: you're on the right track, it is reminding you to be aware of your thoughts and keep a positive state of being, or you can manifest your dreams by the power of thought. Overall, the reason for seeing 12:12 is "to strengthen your confidence to be your true self in a world of people who don't know who you are." Wow!

What 12:12 tells me is that it is time to get over feeling worthless! Return to the Lord and see things from God's perspective. I have to see myself as God sees me. When Jesus was betrayed, He was also considered worthless. The Jewish leaders gave thirty pieces of silver to Judas (who could be any one of us, by the way). That sum of money was considered to be the reimbursement price for the accidental death of a slave

(Exodus 21:32). But Jesus knew, despite what the authorities were implying, that He is priceless in His Father's eyes, and our worth comes not from the world but from the knowing that is within us.

Chapter 7

BEYOND THE BITTERNESS

In Ephesians 4:31–32 (ESV), the apostle Paul tells us,

> Let all bitterness and wrath and anger and clamor and slander be put away from you, along with all malice: and be kind one to another, tenderhearted, forgiving each other, even as God also in Christ forgave you.

WHEN I WAS selected to work at the resort in 1985, which I spoke of earlier, I had my shoulder-length hair all cut off. It would be easier to maintain, and I was yearning for a fresh start. Besides, I had a crush on the woman who did it. She was a bit older than me, and we had met at the Beauty Academy. She was a barber with her own shop on Newbury Street in Boston but needed to be certified and obtain her license to do perms and coloring. I find it ironic that her shop was on the same street where my birth mother had lived when she was pregnant with me. Of course, I had *no* idea about any of that at the time. What I can tell you is that once I had my hair all buzzed off, I felt incredibly liberated—so much so that every time it grew to a length where you could grab any of it, I began to have severe anxiety attacks. I never really questioned it; I would just go get it cut again. One day, I had a "random" encounter at a public-transportation station with an old friend and neighbor of mine. We chatted for a few minutes, and then she seemed to go into a bit of a trancelike state and was staring at me. I felt uncomfortable and asked her what was up. She shook her head as if waking up and told me that she was picturing us as children out at the picnic table in my backyard. She said that it seemed as though every time she and my cousin and I would really start to click and have fun together, a hand would come out of the back door, grab me by the hair, and drag me inside the house.

This was a revelation about where my anxiety attacks were coming from! John 16:13 does promise that the Spirit of Truth will guide us, and even though I had always felt so alone in this world, God had always been right there, hiding in plain sight. I am over sixty years old, and right now, at the time of this writing—more than thirty years later—I am finally able to let my hair grow out. As a girl, I had beautiful long auburn hair with a natural wave, but at that age, I could not appreciate it. There is a woman from my hometown who I run into periodically. It always happens during a time when I need encouragement, and I believe that God has a hand in these "random" or "chance" encounters. She loves to tell me how much of an impression I left on her when she would see me ride my bike past her house with my hair flowing out behind me. It is kind of a shame that I felt the need to cut off the part of me that was so attractive. I did *not* like men seeing me that way, but through her eyes, I learned to embrace my beauty. She is a woman who has endured many trials herself but has a strong and solid faith. This past Easter, I encountered her again at a restaurant that we frequent and where everyone knows us. My partner and I had just been chatting with the hostesses as we waited for our friend to join us for dinner. They commented on my hair and described the color as ash and added that it looked pretty. The younger hostess said that she had once colored her hair to be the color that mine is now. Wow, someone paid money to have what nature has given me. Once our friend arrived, we turned to go to get our seats. There in front of me was that woman from my childhood again with the same story about her memory of me. This time, I was able to share how much it meant to me that she could give me a positive memory about myself. She then told me about her husband having a miraculous healing after suffering a fall recently. I listened intently and agreed that God is good even when we can't see it. She gave my arm a little squeeze as she walked away and told me that I am a good person. I can believe her now because I see myself through a different lens. I pondered why I was so inspired to write about my hair, so I looked up the significance of it and found that the theme is woven throughout the scriptures. It often is tied to a person's identity. Hair does not decompose, so it is a symbol of eternity; and a lock of it was sometimes given as a sign of a promise.

Over the years, God has revealed truths to me in rather mysterious and sometimes-supernatural ways. Like Mary, I have pondered these things in my heart, but I never wanted to share most of them with anyone because it always makes me feel special—having these sacred secrets just between me and God. But now God is nudging me (*hard*, I might say) to give my testimony and share these stories so that others who have suffered in silence might find comfort in knowing they are not alone. Speaking of being alone, sharing the story of my hair and the hand that grabbed me to separate me from my friends reminds me of another time when I was separated from my friends. It seemed like a pattern in my childhood— one that I eventually internalized. It was a sleepover party at my house—the only one I can remember. Any other time I had a friend sleep over, it was usually my cousin, so this group thing was a rare event. As little girls, we were all full of giggles and too wound up to sleep. My mom had come downstairs a few times to hush us, and we would be quiet for a little while, but then the playfulness would reemerge and bring cause for another scolding. This led to me being separated from the group because she made me sleep in another room by myself. After that, everyone quietly went to sleep, but it scared me and imprinted a memory that I can never forget. It taught my subconscious to steer clear of intimate friendships. Heaven forbid that I should let anyone get close enough to really know me. So, as an adult, I moved from friendship to surfacy friendship—even from job to job—without realizing my avoidant tendencies.

Writing this memoir has helped me to take all the pieces of my puzzle out of the box and lay them out on a metaphorical table—a platform where I am starting to see more of the big picture. I know the Spirit is always present, but it is not always visible to me until I see things in retrospect. As the truth becomes clearer, my dilemma is in finding that delicate balance between avoiding "exposing my parent's nakedness" (Genesis 9) like I have all these years and reporting the truth in order to glorify God. I think that intention is the key. I need to focus on the wonderful things that God has done to bring me through all of this rather than focus on all the harm that was done. I must give those negative and bitter emotions their due attention when it becomes appropriate and then move on. Then, and only then, can I keep the pain in the periphery. *The problem I have had in the past is that I never allowed the bitterness to surface, so I was never truly and completely authentic.* I believed the lie that says that if you have nothing nice to say, say nothing at all. That saying may be appropriate in some circumstances, but like any wound that gets covered up, it festers. Mind you, it takes great skill to know how and when to share truths so that bad situations do not accidentally escalate. I think it takes a lifetime of experience of doing it wrong and learning to listen to the Spirit and follow God's timing to master this skill. If any of my story has traces of bitterness, it is because I am still a work in progress. I will move through these emotions in God's good time and not a minute before. It *is* possible to love and honor your parents and hate the things they do/did at the same time! I think Adam S. McHugh has it right when he says on page 189 of his book *Listening Life*, "Anger is an especially difficult emotion for people to deal with constructively, particularly when they have been taught by their families or churches that anger is a sin. I seriously doubt that Jesus overturned the temple tables with a serene religious smile on his face." I totally agree with him, and I am done with apologizing for being human. I also believe that premature or precipitous forgiveness is just a form a denial. Yes, Jesus tells us to forgive "seven times seventy times" in Matthew 18:21–22, *but* it should be done in God's time *after* healing has had a chance to take place by offering our torn-apart hearts to Him to heal. Anything short of this is cutting the grief process short. It does not honor the truth, and it prevents the Holy Spirit from entering us.

TRUTH OR SLANDER?

Martin Luther, and many others, advised, "We are to fear and love God so that we do not tell lies about our neighbors, betray, or slander them, or destroy their reputations. Instead, we are to come to their defense, speak well of them, and interpret everything they do in the best possible light." I want to talk about my family in the best light, and that best light is found in the truth of the Gospel—the Gospel that glorifies God, not humans, and reminds us that we are *all* sinners—each and every one! *No one* is good except God! But because of Jesus—as we confess our shortcomings, expose our weaknesses, and become vulnerable—God can, in equal measure, fill us with grace, and we are given the power to be humble, gentle, lowly, kind, etc., until we are transformed into our own unique versions of the Creator's likeness. Try to remember or learn for the first time the message and the wisdom of Jesus's Sermon on the Mount (Matthew 5–7). "Poor in spirit," in the traditional explanation, means people who recognize their own spiritual poverty—their need for

God. "Blessed are those who mourn" is taken to mean people who repent and mourn over their sins. Let us release the *ego* and finally be honest with ourselves and others about our wounds. Our brokenness and weaknesses are closely linked with our families, friends, and enemies because of our unmet needs. Protecting secrets is admirable but only to a point. *When God speaks to your heart and tells you that it is time for you to share your story for His glory, keeping silent can be an act of disobedience.* When we clear away the clutter of emotions that pretend otherwise—that help us to fake it and say we are OK, we can be left feeling—well, inadequate, disillusioned, less than, empty, and maybe even sad. But remember this: The empty vessels were the ones that were filled with water, and their water was turned into the best wine ever served! So, as we empty our hearts of the things that are no longer helpful, let us allow the Spirit to fill us to the brim and even until we overflow. May we be so full of goodness that the demons never return. May we be washed clean and made ready for the great banquet and the return of the Messiah!

RETURNING LIKE QUAN YIN

An old family friend read an earlier version of this manuscript and shared his opinions about my writing. He advised that I use softer word choices and come across less bitter. That will all come in time, but for now, my genuine feelings need to work their way out in God's time. For now, I must be honest and say that at times, especially after learning new details of my story that he shared (ones that I will discuss in a moment), suffice it to say that I am *as mad as a hive of angry bees*! He also advised that I elaborate on the details of my stories, and to that, I wholeheartedly agree. So, first and foremost, I want to tell you about Quan Yin, a bodhisattva of great compassion. Her legend closely ties to my life's story. In the Buddhist tradition, "a bodhisattva is a human being that has made a vow to dedicate their lifetimes to the enlightenment of all humankind. Bodhisattvas continue to reincarnate and return to the world to help guide others to enlightenment." So let me tell you how I learned about her.

All my life, as a child and as an adult, I longed to see my dad stand up to my mother. He finally did when he gave me a statue that had been his father's, my grandfather's, and it was special to me because it had been special to him. We were gathered around the family dining table during one of the holidays, and the subject of idols came up. My mom used the Buddha as an example and stated that she was uncomfortable with having it in her home. I knew that a hunk of metal was not an idol but rather anything that you hold more sacred than God—be it money, a relationship, a child, an addiction, etc. Those are idols. My mother's obsession with food was an idol, but my grandfather's statue was not one. I told my dad that I would like to have it if he was just going to throw it out. I was an adult at this point and had a home of my own. My dad got up from the table, went into the living room, brought it back to the table, and simply placed it down in front of me. That was a moment I am eternally grateful for! My brother's husband then proceeded to tell us, "That is not Buddha. Her name is Quan Yin." I thought she was so cool because she, like me, chose to return to the chaos and to be of service.

Years earlier, at my eldest brother's request, I chose to return. I had taken a job in the mountains of New Hampshire, and it was just before Christmas when I had second thoughts about spending my life going to work at one resort after another. I had been referred to work there by the director of the resort I had worked at in 1985 and 1987, and I figured that I could just keep getting referrals to work at other resorts from there. After an incident that involved maintenance coming into my room without asking, I realized I couldn't just run away. I realized that the boundaries were up to me to maintain and that there would always be someone who would break them if I allowed it. I needed to find a better way of dealing with these issues. So I called home and spoke with my eldest brother about it all, and he said, *"Come home. We'll fix this."* I should tell you that just a few years earlier, I had asked him if he thought that our dad had abused me as an infant. He flipped out! He accused me of thinking that I was so attractive that not even my father could resist me. *How ridiculous, I thought. A baby can't be attractive in that way, and why did my question elicit such a strong response?* At the time, I just put it all on the back burner to ponder it and dropped it, but now he was inviting me to revisit the issues at hand. I sometimes wonder if he had witnessed anything about my abuse and felt guilty in some way for not protecting me. That could have played into why he repetitively engaged in such high-risk sexual encounters, which eventually led to his dying of AIDS. I'll never know for sure about that, but I was so grateful that he invited me to come home that I quit my job and returned to the family to get things fixed. *What we did not know was that the thing that needed fixing might have begun before I was adopted but after my birth mother relinquished me.* This is the thing that I am angry about! Our old family friend shared information with me and told me a story that my mother had shared with him many years ago. She told him that I had been sexually abused as an infant before they adopted me. She told him that social services had investigated the family and deemed them to be safe, so they placed me with them. I have reason to believe that while that may be true, it may also be true that she was attempting to either cover up or possibly confess the abuse that I suffered while I was in her care. I like facts, so I went back to the network that helped me to find my birth mother with this information. I am waiting to see what details are in my files about this preadoption abuse. *Regardless of the outcome, the point is this: God gave me the ability—the grace—to care for my parents in their old age. At the time I was tasked with this responsibility, I truly believed that they had abused me.* It really hurt that they were fine with me hating myself because of it. But God gave me *more* grace—*amazing*!

I will give my dad credit because one time, he broke down in tears in front of me, thinking that I could never forgive him. He was sobbing, and at the time, I had no idea why, but I told him that I *had* forgiven him a thousand times and that I would forgive him another thousand times, but none of that mattered unless he learned to forgive himself! A few years later, when I realized what he was crying about, he agreed to go with me to talk things out with a family minister/psychologist. My mom put the kibosh on that, so we all stayed stuck. In my mom's defense, I do believe that in her own unique way, she tried to encourage my healing and left me some breadcrumbs to follow as I journeyed along my path to healing. She gave me a book, and when she did, my instincts told me that there was more to this gift than met the eye. The book was Sue Monk Kidd's *The Secret Life of Bees*. The story is about a young girl who escapes her father's abuse and finds a group of sisters who share a heritage of abuse; they were abused just for being Black in South Carolina in 1964. They teach her female power—the real kind that seeks *no* revenge. They shared with her their reverence for the Black Madonna. The protagonist learns to believe in herself and, by example, helped me to do the same. I don't think my mother knew any other way to help me escape the mental prison that she had put me in. She had also given me two small plates that had bees and dragonflies on them. I still use them to this day and smile knowingly every time I do.

The self-loathing was *by far* more detrimental than any physical/sexual abuse, but the blame should *not* fall completely on my parents. Society has come a long way in recognizing the signs and symptoms of abuse, and there are now many resources that can help both victims and abusers, but we have a *long* way to go in creating safe spaces for children! Children and adults need to be able to speak their truths without fear of retaliation against themselves *or* against their family members. *For many years, I held in these toxic secrets because I did not want any harm to come to the people I loved—even though they had hurt me.* So if you're reading this and you get the urge to hate anyone that I have described to you in these pages, please *stop*! God forgave you, so find it in your heart to forgive—not condone by *any measure* but forgive. Give it to God because vengeance is His. The Creator can take all these trials and tribulations and make something of great beauty from it all!

A devotional I read recently advises us not to "freeze people in time," meaning that if you run into someone from your past, give them the benefit of the doubt and the opportunity to show you that they have grown since you last knew them. But be realistic and not naive or cloud your vision with wishful thinking. Worse yet, not seeing clearly can keep toxic secrets alive and well. A friend recently commented during our Bible study that one should "believe but validate." When I was told about my alleged preadoption abuse, it caused me to go back and reanalyze everything. I realized that there was so much more about my early years that I had not thought too much about but most certainly helped to shape me and validate the things that I believe God shared with me regarding my parents. In the spirit of truth, for clarity, and to investigate the facts, let me now share the parts of my story I have not yet told you. I have seven of these short little narratives.

1. Labeled

When I was still in high school, like many girls, I was being pressured to have sex. I broke up with many of my boyfriends, and some broke up with me over this issue. I was not about to give in to some horny teenager! I did, however, wonder what I was missing out on, so I was open to experimenting should the right situation present itself. I know that does not sound very Christian, but at that time in my life, my focus was not on the dos and don'ts that are in the scriptures. We had foreign-exchange students from Japan one summer before my senior year of high school and were enjoying an outing at the local roller-skating arena when I met him—the one I chose to give myself to. He was a bit older than me, tall, dark, and very handsome, but what attracted me the most was his calm and mature nature. He had been married for a short time—until he and his wife lost their young son to a genetic disease. It devastated their marriage. When I met him while roller-skating, he was at a crossroads in his life, so we were perfect together while it lasted. I won't go into all the intimate details of our relationship, but I will say that thanks to him, I don't hate men. For a while, my parents were suspicious of our relationship and why this young man was so interested in me. In time, I got tired of the constant questioning and spilled the beans. They were too late, I said. My mom got all flustered and asked me what I meant. But my dad blurted out his thoughts and called me a name no father should ever call his daughter! Now that I look back, he had quite the nerve to say that to me. In any case, the relationship ended when my lover was transferred to another Coast Guard station, and I never saw him again. My heart was broken, but no one seemed to care, so I started thinking that perhaps my dad was right. For several years after that, I proceeded to live up to what he had called me and lived a wild and promiscuous life until I realized that the lifestyle just did not fit me. I was *not* what

HELLO, MY NAME IS GRACE

he had accused me of; I was just a normal, red-blooded girl. Eventually, I met my life partner and settled down with her. Just before we moved in together, my family made a trip to San Francisco to visit my sister, who was living there at the time. Her children flew in, as well as me with my parents, and we all had theater tickets to see *The Nutcracker*. That afternoon, to pass the time as we waited for the show, my dad and I took a trolley ride and wound up at a maritime museum at the trolley driver's suggestion. Who do you think was our tour guide? You guessed it—Mr. Tall, Dark, and Handsome! My dad was very uncomfortable with the whole situation, which, I must admit, made it even more fun for me. As for my ex, I needed to see him again to realize that our breakup was the best thing for me. It was God saying "*No*, you can't have him" because he had something much better in mind for me. I was happy to have closure and was ready to move on without any regrets.

2. Overpowering the Enemy

We were having one of our usual family gatherings at my parents' house. It was a cookout and a pool party, and my cousin's creepy husband was there. I guess men being men brings out the worst in them, and Dad decided to act in a way that made me sick. We were in the pool, and I had had enough of the inappropriateness for one day. He did something that got under my skin, so I blocked him, grabbed both of his wrists, and bent his arms back just far enough to let him know that I could really hurt him if I wanted to. A look of terror appeared on his face. I stared at him without saying a word, dropped his wrists, and emphatically left the pool. That was the last time he *ever* treated me that way. Many years later, while he was watching me play softball, a conversation with my teammates caused him to confess that he had been afraid of me for years—to which I responded, "As you should be." The adrenaline rush and release that I felt after saying those words was almost overwhelming. It was my turn to bat, and I was *so* very grateful for the opportunity to release my emotions on that poor ball. I had one of my best hits ever.

3. My Sister's Bridesmaid

When my sister was planning her wedding, I remember thinking that I never wanted to go through all the hassles she was experiencing. There was a certain sense of excitement, I will admit. She was happy and looking forward to her big day. I agreed to be one of her bridesmaids and even wear one of the dresses she had picked out for all of us. It was a big deal for me as I almost never wore anything other than jeans or chinos. I didn't even like wearing shorts all that much because looking girlish or showing my legs in public made me feel too vulnerable. I must admit, I did have good-looking legs from all my bicycle riding and from being on the swim team. Now that I'm older, the veins are showing up, but I still have the muscle tone, LOL! So let's go back to the wedding plans. I was included in the meetings with the maid of honor, and one day, she shared something with me that I will be forever grateful for. She let me know how badly my mother spoke of me behind my back. I was old enough at this time to hear that news and not be devastated by it. It helped me to see through much of the gaslighting that my siblings and I were starting to figure out. It also made me wonder why my mom needed to make me out to be some sort of villain. I started to sift through and reanalyze all the lies and half-truths I believed about myself. My sister's maid of honor, in a strange way, gave me back my honor.

4. Their Reaction, or Lack Thereof

Many years later, my sister's marriage ended in divorce. It was no wonder because her husband was a two-timer and a predator. He eventually ran off with her best friend and had two more children but not before he attempted to violate me. When I turned eighteen, I went on a trip to visit my sister out of state. I was excited to be of legal drinking age there and was looking forward to ordering a drink when we all went out to dinner together. Just before we headed out, my sister, who was suffering from pregnancy-related issues, decided not to go. She sent her husband and me out so that we could enjoy ourselves. Dinner was great, and I felt all grown-up. Afterward, her husband suggested stopping at a nightclub, and in my naivety, I agreed. There was a man in that club who was a little too interested in me, and I was uncomfortable. My sister's husband thought it would be a good idea for us to pretend to be a couple so that the man would leave me alone. It sounded good, so I went along with it. It worked, and the man left, but the couple act didn't stop. I told her husband to knock it off and take me home. All the way there, he was hitting on me, so I attempted to jump out of the car. He apologized, drove us home, and made himself comfortable in his favorite chair when we got back to their house. I went right to bed in the guest room after making sure to close the door tightly. I woke up to him being on top of me. I could only think of my sister and how betrayed she would feel as I threw him off me and scolded him. Neither of us spoke of it until I opened my mouth many years later. My parents were blaming my sister for the divorce, saying she didn't try hard enough as a wife. I piped up with "Wait one minute—there is something you should all know about Mr. Wonderful," and I told them what he had done. I half-hoped to get a little empathy for what I had suffered, but I mostly just wanted to defend my sister. My parents stopped blaming her but *never* showed me any compassion whatsoever. I found this to be a bit odd, so I asked my sister how she would have responded if her daughter had shared that information with her. She assured me that our parents' response was, at best, a bit cold.

5. My Brother's Health Proxy

On the night that my brother died of AIDS, my partner and I had gone shopping for our nieces' and nephews' birthday gifts because many of them were born in August. We also made sure we had funeral clothes because we wanted to be ready for the inevitable. We were all set up and went out to the front steps to have a smoke. Yes, I am a former smoker and not proud of that fact, and quitting was the hardest thing I ever did. Anyhow, as we sat on the steps and smoked, I looked up to the stars and said to the universe—and to my brother—that I was ready for him to pass. The phone rang immediately. It was my other brother calling us into town; it was time! An ancestor of my eldest brother, a woman who looked like a pilgrim, had been haunting the house that both brothers were now living in. She was there when the younger brother and his husband bought it, and she was always at the top of the stairwell that led to the back door. When the one with AIDS got really sick, the other moved him into their rental unit on the first floor. The ghost moved to the bottom of that stairwell—just outside his apartment door. After he was put in hospice care, she moved to the corner of his bedroom, and his friend and caretaker could not only sense her presence but could also see her! On the night that my brother died, she had moved to the foot of his bed. That's where she was when I arrived and got into the bed with him. I lay with him for a long time while the family was gathered around and finally got up to go out and have a smoke. The minute I lit up my cigarette, they called me back inside. He had passed, and his ghost friend was gone too. One of the "family" members present was his good friend and health proxy. We went outside to talk at his request, and he asked me if there had ever been any abuse in our family. I told him that I could describe the "fruits" of our family and that he could tell me what he thought the tree was. I gave him examples like I am sharing with you now. He breathed a sigh of relief, hugged me tight, and said "Thank you." He needed validation for what his gut had been telling him for years. He said that every time he would attempt to bring up the subject, my brother's eyes would glaze over, and he would say robotically that he was so lucky to have been adopted. I hope and pray that my brother's ghost friend was an agent of God and that she was able to get through his defenses and lead him out of denial and back to paradise.

6. Afraid That I Would Care for Her the Way She Cared for Me

The task of caring for my parents seemed so unfair at the time, but I trusted that God knew what She was doing in assigning that responsibility to me. The assisted-living facility that they had moved into after Mom broke her hip was a blessing to all of us—even to me—always validating me and helping me to navigate her narcissism. I loved that my dad was free of his "Honey, do … " list and was really enjoying his time with the other residents. My aunt, my mom's sister, was also living there in the dementia unit, so I would frequently see her daughter, my cousin. She loved reporting to me how it also brought her joy to see my dad so happy; she had even seen him skipping down a corridor on his way to play pool with one of his new friends. Unfortunately, my mom did not share this joy. She apparently told many of my relatives how much she missed her home, which was understandable. I would miss my home too if I were in that situation. But she took it to another level when she attempted to sabotage my caregiving. I ended up having my partner and the facility double-check *everything* I did so that I could be sure that I was not subconsciously retaliating. When I was sure that I was *not* doing that, I addressed the issue with her. I asked, "Mom, are you afraid that I will take care of you the way you took care of me?" She could not look at me, so I said, "Jesus would *never* let me do that." That was that, and she began to trust me. Ultimately, as I told you before, she was able to have a relatively peaceful passing, and for that, I am eternally grateful. The only way to defeat evil is to overcome it with goodness and love (Romans 12:21 NIV). There's that *twelve* again!

7. What Is "It"?

After my parents had both passed and my remaining brother and his husband returned from their world cruise, we settled all the financial and burial affairs. Both parents wanted to be cremated, so that made it possible for us to wait and bury them on what would have been their sixty-sixth wedding anniversary. There were only a handful of us at the grave site—my mom's remaining sister and her now-deceased brother's widow with whom she was very close. My siblings and I were there with our partners, and I was asked to perform the ceremonies. It was my honor. I was respectful but honest and felt that God smiled on us all that day. Some time afterward, or maybe it was just days before the funeral, my brother and his husband stopped our conversation and asked me what was the "it" that I referred to from time to time. I told them the story of how God had shown me in 1985 what the secret was. They both nodded in agreement and said that they had always known there was something but could not quite put their finger on it.

DRAGONFLY SYMBOLISM

That reminds me, I need to tell you the other part of the story with the dragonfly! Many years after all of this took place, I found a new church community that had ties to my childhood church but was much healthier for me. I was ready, so God revealed a neat little detail about my dragonfly. Let me start by telling you about my tattoo. After I had met my birth mother, I needed a little space to clear my head, so I went away by myself to a bed-and-breakfast near the resort where I had worked in 1985. On my way home, I drove by a tattoo shop, and the Spirit moved me to turn around and go inside. I talked to a young man who explained to me that the owner, Buck, was not in that day, so I would need to come back. That suited me just fine because I needed to discuss the idea with my partner and wanted time to think things over. I made an appointment to get my dragonfly tattoo, and the evening before, I was invited to an impromptu backyard barbeque at our friend Holly's house. I was telling her that I was going to get my first (and only) tattoo the next day, and they asked me where I was going to have it done. Mind you, the party I was at was in Massachusetts, but the tattoo shop was in

New Hampshire, and I told them that they wouldn't know the guy. To my surprise, they *all* knew Buck, and most of them had been tattooed by him! They all showed me his work, and I saw body parts I should not have seen, but *wow*—this sure reassured me that I was doing the right thing. I got my tattoo and loved it. Buck focused on and depicted more of the dragonfly's body than the wings, and I thought that was super cool because I find bugs fascinating. God has since revealed to me why he used the dragonfly to comfort me. He told me to look at the structure of my dragonfly and imagine its legs all raised in praise to Him and compare it to the menorah, the seven lamps that are symbolic of the sevenfold Spirit of God, which is mentioned in both Isaiah 11, a prophecy foretelling the incarnation of Jesus, and in Revelation 4, which readies us for his return. These are the seven spirits of God: wisdom, counsel, knowledge, fear of the Lord, might, understanding, and the Lord/Yahweh at the center. Below are some pictures so you can see for yourself and the scripture verses. Jesus began his ministry by stating that He was here to fulfill the prophecy in Isaiah (Luke 4:2).

> The Spirit of the LORD will rest on him—
> the Spirit of wisdom and of understanding,
> the Spirit of counsel and of might,

the Spirit of the knowledge and fear of the LORD. (Isaiah 11:2 NIV)

From the throne came flashes of lightning, rumblings, and peals of thunder. In front of the throne, seven lamps were blazing. These are the seven of God. (Revelation 4:5 NIV)

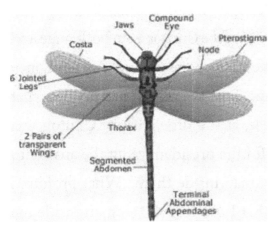 

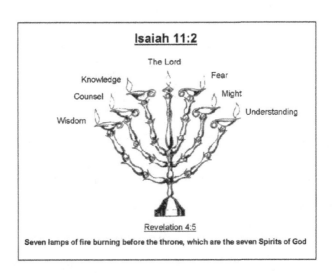

Isaiah 11:2

Seven lamps of fire burning before the throne, which are the seven Spirits of God

> And we all, who with unveiled faces contemplate
> the LORD's glory, are being transformed into his
> image with ever-increasing glory, which comes
> from the LORD, who is the Spirit. (2 Corinthians
> 3:18 NIV)

My life's path has always led me to try and emulate my hero, Jesus. I read this scripture and think, *I am "trans"—transitioning into the likeness of the Creator.* I am both male and female and created in the very image of God. A friend once asked me what women men fear the most. I had no idea what he was getting at because, at the time, Hillary Clinton was running against Trump for the presidency. But the answer to who they fear is "the woman inside them." What profound wisdom! I have to say that I too fear the woman inside me because she is weak and vulnerable. I also fear the man that is inside of me because he is aggressive and self-seeking and can be destructive. But Jesus—Jesus is the perfect combination— the perfect balance of God-fearing masculinity with the tenderness and caring of a woman. That is why He is my hero—not just because of His salvation and what He did for me on the cross but because of the example He shows me. Many times, when I have struggled to forgive, I look to Him and His final words: "Father, forgive them, for they know not what they do." If He could suffer the way He did and have that response, I have no excuses. I repetitively commend my spirit to God, hoping that I'll fly back to heaven and live with Jesus there, but apparently, it is not my time yet. I hope that sharing my story with you has helped you in some small way. Perhaps this is the reason that I am still here.

Chapter 8

YES!

> For no matter how many promises
> God has made, they are "Yes" in Christ.
> And so, through him the "Amen" is
> spoken by us to the glory of God.
> —2 Corinthians 1:20 (NIV)

BRICK BY BRICK—TAKE ME TO CHURCH

JOURNALIST DAVID BRINKLEY is quoted as saying, "A successful person is the one who can lay a firm foundation with the bricks others have thrown at them." One of my bricks came from the church I was raised in. The church's district leader (bishop) tried to teach the congregation that it was their Christian duty to deny me communion (and therefore salvation) based on my choice of life partner. The idea was that I would come to my senses and admit that loving my partner was a sin. I believe that God had brought us together, so my story played out in a way that made many reexamine what they understood about the scriptures and, perhaps, the very nature of God. I had tried to find a partner of the opposite sex to have children with (children I would most likely have abused or neglected), but instead, I found someone who brought forth my own inner child. The process was painful, but it also deepened my faith. God does indeed work in mysterious ways. Like what happened to Joseph in the Bible, betrayal by your own family can, if handled properly, help you to grow. It is your choice to take God's hand or to try to walk it out on your own power. God always has a plan for you and waits patiently for you to trust Him. Psalm 27:10 (NASB) says, "For my father and my mother have forsaken me, but the Lord will take me in." That verse opened a door for me. In all the world, what can be better than that? To be able to really know deep in your soul and then say "God is my father and my mother" is a privilege worth struggling for. I realized how well God knows me and how deeply He loves me. He had a plan from the beginning to lead me out of the darkness and into His glorious light—not only for my sake but also for the sake of the countless people whom I would be able to relate to and help in the future. I was and will always be a soldier in His army. People sign up for service in the military and expect it to be difficult but meaningful and worthwhile. Freedom is always worth the fight, and winning the battle for your mind is the most rewarding one. Perhaps the day of peace will come soon—when war is no more. The wars that men fight all begin with the war inside, and it is the most difficult to master. In John 16:12–13 (LSB), Jesus says, "I have many more things to say to you, but you cannot bear them now. But when he, the Spirit of truth comes, he will guide you into all truth." The secret secrets are the ones you keep from yourself, and only the Holy Spirit can show you the way out of the deception and isolation.

Doing things that are countercultural can attract quite a few bricks. When I volunteered to ride from Boston to New York City in 1995, the folks in Bridgeport, Connecticut, literally threw stones and bricks at some of the riders. My brother was dying of AIDS, and my mom had asked me if I could do this 360-mile bicycle ride for him. At the time, society was so fearful and was of the mindset that this disease was God's way of eliminating homosexuals. That included many hospitals and churches, but we would *not* listen! There were about 1,500 riders plus all the crew that it required to raise money. More importantly, we raised spirits and awareness about those suffering from the illness as well as their loved ones who suffered along with them.

Bricks are also part of the liberation story found in Exodus 5—when Moses approached the Pharaoh to say, "Thus says the Lord, the God of Israel, let my people go." The king of

Egypt responded by making the slaves work harder by adding the chore of gathering the straw needed to make the bricks. I too experienced something similar in my corporate position when I defended the union laborers against the derogatory, dismissive, and fearful view that management took of them. It ultimately led me to resign, take another job and lose it, and end up in this place of being free from employment—where I have the privilege and honor of writing this book and sharing my story with you. God truly does work all things together for the good of those who love Him (Romans 8:28 NIV)!

So if God is for us, who can be against us (Romans 8:31 NIV)? Acts 20:21 compels us to return to God. When you see our Creator the way He *truly* is, rather than through the erroneous depictions that people throughout the ages have made up, your heart will leap for joy—like a long-lost friend who runs to Him as He runs to you. See the story in Luke 15:11–32. It is an awesome invitation. We need to step out of the shadows of fear and into the light—the wonderful, pure, unadulterated, sustainable, and glorious light of Jesus Christ!

Into the light! Plato is quoted as having said, "We can easily forgive a child who is afraid of the dark; the real tragedy of life is when men are afraid of the light." Many people are at least a little "afraid of the light" because it means that we must change. As much as most people complain, most of us find some strange comfort in our less-than-ideal lives, our less-than-best selves, and our less-than-what-God-would-have-for-us way of being. It takes trust to leave the boat and walk out onto the water! Trust that Jesus will sustain us when we fail because He died to give us the freedom to try. We are free to learn from our mistakes without condemnation. By the way, if our abusers repent, that goes for them too! Romans 8:1 (ASV) tells us, "There is therefore now no condemnation for those who are in Christ Jesus." The devil loves to point out our flaws so he can rub our noses in them. The Holy Spirit loves to bring them to our attention but only so that we can get clean again and be free—free to love God with everything we have and then love one another as we long to be loved. It is in the giving of love that we receive it.

Speaking of the devil—or, as some would say, the dragon or tempter—I have a car magnet, a T-shirt, and a hat that say, "Not today, Satan. Not today." They remind me not to yield to that little bastard! At the abbey where I did the bulk of this literary work, I purchased a simple necklace with a key-shaped medallion on it. Not having been raised Catholic, I had no idea which saint was on it. I just liked the idea of the key because it reminds me that in Christ, I am free. It turns out that the medallion is of Saint Benedict, the father of monastic life, and it has on its back in the shape of a cross "CSSML—NDSMD," which are acronyms for the Latin sayings that translate to "May the holy cross be my light! May the dragon never be my overlord!" Surrounding the back of the medal are the letters "VRSNSMV—SMQLIVB," which mean, "Be gone, Satan! Never tempt me with your vanities! What you offer me is evil. Drink the poison yourself!" Furthermore, Revelation 13:16–17 (ISV) warns us about the time when we will not be able to buy or sell without the mark of the beast—the proverbial mark of the devil. But I say, refuse it! Walk in faith instead—even if it kills you. I believe that with freedom as the alternative, you are *way* better off. It is a journey that can be frightening, but you are never alone. God assures us of His presence in both the old and new covenants—in both Deuteronomy 31:8 and Hebrews 13:5.

Some say that things do not end well for those of us who are daring enough to be countercultural. But I am reminded by the scriptures that those courageous people end up on the right-hand side of God. I suppose that it depends on which life you are trying to preserve—this momentary, guaranteed-to-end-in-death-anyway one or your eternal life. Look at the stories of Isaac and of Christ; they were willing sacrifices and lay down their lives in faith, for God's glory is the whole point of the scriptures and what Jesus calls us to do as His disciples. I am by no means advocating recklessness of any kind. This daringness must come from one's obedience to the Holy Spirit and not from one's own "thimbleful of understanding." I heard that expression while listening to a sermon by Paul

Sheppard when he preached about Abram and Sarai before they were renamed Abraham and Sarah. He was describing their plan to make God's plan come to fruition with their own power—a human plan that resulted in the birth of Ishmael and a consequence that is still playing out in today's political landscape. I find that it is always best to wait on the Lord.

The Spirit will lead, and grace gives us the strength to succeed if we embrace it. As it says in Ephesians 4:12 (NIV), "To equip his people for works of service, so that the body of Christ may be built up," the goal being the attainment of spiritual maturity, as in verse 13, "the measure of the stature of the fullness of Christ." Remember that having either too high or too low an opinion of oneself is equally off the mark when it comes to truth and reality. The reality is that we are all God's children—flawed but loved just the same because of who God is. Humility is the great equalizer that keeps our view of ourselves and others in perspective—in line with God's perspective of truth. As for self-worth, the scriptures remind me in 1 Corinthians 1:28 (ASV) that "the base things of the world, and the things that are despised, did God choose, yea and the things that are not, that he might bring to naught the things that are."

If all of this reads like a Hallmark movie, perhaps it is because my mother's maiden name is Hall; therefore, I also am a Hall. It's the name on my otherwise blank birth certificate.

Whether or not you believe any part of this memoir of mine, I ask only that you pray for me and anyone struggling for any reason with their identity. My aim is to turn my tests into a testimony. On my own, I am, like everyone else, powerless over sin and the devil. All glory and honor be to Christ, for if not but by His grace, just like Paul says in 1 Corinthians 15:10. This book is my story of transformation and redemption; it is my mark and God's mark on me and Satan's failed attempt to mark me. Praise God! It *is* a Hall-mark. As for my other name—Shepherd—that comes from my birth father.

The Lord instructs us to "offer God a sacrifice of thanksgiving! Fulfill the promises you made to the Most High! Cry out to me whenever you are in trouble; I will deliver you, then you will honor me" (Psalm 50:14–15 CEB). My praise is accepting the name that God gave me when no one else wanted me. Thanks be to Papa! I am ready to be who the Creator made me to be. Send me out into the harvest! *Let Your light shine and let us come to know that we all bear Your holy name.* I believe that the whole purpose of creation—the who, what, where, and why of it all—is for us to reach full maturity or, as Maslow calls it, self-actualization. I wonder what full-blown love will look like? What will it be like when we stop hurting ourselves and one another?

RETURN ON INVESTMENT—FAREWELL LETTER

In 2020, I was hired and let go of yet another job, but this one was different. First off, I was seeing things much more clearly (how ironic that it happened in 2020—you know, 20/20 vision). I was in a position where I had a global audience. My team was made up of a diverse group of engineers and professionals, and inside, I did not have the confidence to be there, but God got me through each and every day. I placed a stone on the dashboard of my car with an inscription of Psalm 118—"This is the day that the Lord has made"—to remind me of the Creator's presence. Each morning, I was tasked to lead the executive team meeting, and at first, it was quite nerve-racking, but it gave me the stage to shine. In the end, I was asked to train my replacements in our overseas offices when the company restructured and closed the local branch. I was told by many of my colleagues how much of a difference I made in their lives. I may not have had extensive job knowledge, but I do know people. There were two angels on the team that I supervised, and they got me through those difficult days. They were two women who were hired through a temp agency in Kuala Lumpur, Malaysia. They both had such great work ethics, but more than that, they were true team players and had servant hearts. Even though they had a totally different culture, spoke a different language, and were of a different religion, we became like sisters. We listened to one another and worked together to find solutions to our work problems as well as some personal issues that were work-related. In our own unique and diverse ways, we prayed and supported one another, and we continue to do so to this very day. I only hope that the company can see their true value beyond their ability to increase the bottom line. Because of them and many other coworkers that I cared deeply about, I was moved to write a letter to the entire global team before I left. Here is a copy of my parting thoughts, which many people, including the head of HR, thanked me for writing and sending out:

> **Departure Note (11.18.2022)** Thank you all for this wonderful opportunity to learn and grow. These past two years have been quite an experience. I have met a lot of wonderful people. Been encouraged, but also suffered extreme self-doubts. I have been incapacitated to the point of needing a wheelchair for mobility, with its subsequent spinal surgery. And, most recently, been diagnosed with an autoimmune disease that caused great difficulty in daily activity, so much so, that it was difficult to even dress myself. But my biggest challenge was that I had to learn to "play in the sandbox" and learn to

let go of control, after having spent nineteen years fully responsible for my environment at my previous employment. It was not an easy transition. I want you to know that you all have assisted me in your own unique way, and for that, I am truly grateful.

My thoughts to leave you with as we journey on into the great unknown:

1. Remember to see difficulties as opportunities.
2. Be conscious of who and what you serve. In the end, we cannot take any of this with us. Nothing matters more than the relationships we build along the way.

   As a customer service industry, and individually, my hope is that we all come to choose love ♡ above all else, and thus inherit The Kingdom! There is no better ROI.

Peace Out ✌🕊

JUST SAY YES!

"Later, as Jesus left the town, he saw a tax collector named Levi sitting at his tax collector's booth. 'Follow me and be my disciple,' Jesus said to him. So Levi got up, left everything, and followed him" (Luke 5:27–28 NLT). Why would Levi (Matthew) make such a drastic decision so suddenly? Why would anyone risk so much in an instant? As a tax collector, Levi knew how to make money, but perhaps he longed for an opportunity to make a difference. Levi had a certain authority that was granted by the Romans, but perhaps what he really wanted was that special anointing—the one granted only by God. Levi was probably quite sufficient materially, but perhaps he was aware of the deep deficiencies in his spirit.

"A sober recognition of who we are is precisely what makes the person God invites us to become, so compelling. Prayer: Lord, help me say yes to you ... right now. Amen."[2]

We are called to a Christian community, which focuses on interdependence rather than independence. Communities of faith are not so much about pulling oneself up by the bootstraps but about working together to provide boots for those who have none and to help one another put them on. Proverbs 31:8–9 (NIV) reads, "Speak up for those who cannot speak for themselves, for the rights of all who are destitute. Speak up and judge fairly; defend the rights of the poor and needy." Telling my story is my attempt to speak when others may not have yet found their voices. My hope is to encourage

---

[2] Borrowed from UCC Devotional *New Life ... in an Instant* by Kenneth L. Samuel, published on January 21, 2023.

anyone who may be struggling with any of these issues. The following was inspiring to me:

"Advent (and every other day) is also a good time to be an encourager, an affirmer to others. In a women's group, we spoke about 'Elizabething' one another; that is, affirming God's call in each other just as Elizabeth did to Mary. We don't always have a clear sense of our own callings, and it's helpful to have others tell us what they see in us."[3]

MARY VISITS ELIZABETH (LUKE 1:39–45 NIV)

At that time Mary got ready and hurried to a town in the hill country of Judea, where she entered Zechariah's home and greeted Elizabeth. When Elizabeth heard Mary's greeting, the baby leaped in her womb, and Elizabeth was filled with the Holy Spirit. In a loud voice, she exclaimed: "Blessed are you among women, and blessed is the child you will bear! But why am I so favored, that the mother of my LORD should come to me? As soon as the sound of your greeting reached my ears, the baby in my womb leaped for joy. Blessed is she who has believed that the LORD would fulfill his promises to her!"

Mary said "Yes."

See her song of praise.

---

[3] Taken from https://www.womenoftheelca.org/blog/daily-grace/be-an-elizabeth-this-advent.

THE MAGNIFICAT (LUKE 1:46–55 NIV)

And Mary said:

"My soul glorifies the LORD

and my spirit rejoices in God my Savior,

for he has been mindful

of the humble state of his servant.

From now on all generations will call me blessed,

for the Mighty One has done great things for me—

holy is his name.

His mercy extends to those who fear him,

from generation to generation.

He has performed mighty deeds with his arm;

he has scattered those who are proud in their

inmost thoughts.

He has brought down rulers from their thrones

but has lifted up the humble.

He has filled the hungry with good things

but has sent the rich away empty.

He has helped his servant Israel,

remembering to be merciful

to Abraham and his descendants forever,

just as he promised our ancestors."

Notice that after Mary has been affirmed by her cousin
Elizabeth in her knowledge of carrying the Divine within her

body, she breaks into a song of exultation and a declaration of God's concern for justice. Justice will be established in a radical way—through God's love in sending Jesus. Spend time on thinking about what a revolutionary message Mary proclaimed. Imagine how you fit into this proclamation.

> For Zion's sake I will not keep silent, and for Jerusalem's sake I will not be quiet, until her righteousness goes forth as brightness, and her salvation as a burning torch.
>
> The nations shall see your righteousness, and all the kings your glory, and you shall be called by a new name that the mouth of the LORD will give.
>
> You shall be a crown of beauty in the hand of the LORD, and a royal diadem in the hand of your God. You shall no more be termed Forsaken, and your land shall no more be termed Desolate, but you shall be called My Delight Is in Her, and your land Married; for the LORD delights in you, and your land shall be married. For as a young man marries a young woman, so shall your sons marry you, and as the bridegroom rejoices over the bride, so shall your God rejoice over you. (Isaiah 62:1–5 ESV)

Yep, you read that right—the Creator wants to marry you! But He wants to marry the real you, the you who is free from all that would weigh you down—the you who is acquitted of any wrongdoing and who is free to love and serve and be served. Can you imagine such a world? If you're worried that you are not worthy, just remember this: "Whoever has ears, let them hear what the Spirit says to the churches. To the one who is victorious, I will give some of the hidden manna. I will also give that person a white stone with a new name written on it, known only to the one who receives it" (Revelation 2:17 NIV).

So now you know my story and how I came to know my true, God-given identity. We all have scripts that were programmed into us from childhood, were reinforced throughout life, and conform to our individual cultures. My culture centers on Jesus, but love shows up in a million ways. My dream is to see the Creator's dream come to full fruition, and I see Jesus returning by manifesting fully within each of us. God has named each of us. *My God-given name is Grace; what is yours?*

Epilogue

Truly, my life's story shows that there was "honey in the rock" (Psalm 81:16 NIV). Sweet blessings were born in hard times and during some of my greatest challenges.

The law of attraction might suggest that a feeling or belief that one is worthless will attract negative experiences. While that can be and frequently is true, it is also true that my neediness has attracted the Creator like an *enormous* magnet! My weakness draws His healing powers like blood draws sharks but *more so* because behind the wound is a little girl crying out to Papa. The Creator responded by showing me where my injury was the greatest—that of having not been named and a deep sense of not being wanted or appreciated for who I *am*.

Again, just say, *"Yes, I am created in the image of the I Am!"*

"A sober recognition of who we are is precisely what makes the person God invites us to become, so compelling."[4]

---

[4] Borrowed from UCC Devotional *New Life … in an Instant* by Kenneth L. Samuel, published on January 21, 2023.

You might be thinking, *What is the big deal? Why is a name so important?* Well, this is what Jesus had to say about the power of the name: "I have revealed your name to the men you gave me out of the world. They belonged to you, and you gave them to me, and they have obeyed your word" (John 17:6 NET).

"When I was with them, I kept them safe and watched over them in your name that you have given me. Not one of them was lost except the one destined for destruction, so that the scripture could be fulfilled. But now I am coming to you, and I am saying these things in the world, so they may experience my joy completed in themselves" (John 17:12 NET).

"Righteous Father, even if the world does not know you, I know you, and these men know that you sent me. I made known your name to them, and I will continue to make it known, so that the love you have loved me with may be in them, and I may be in them" (John 17:25–26 NET).

- Remember that God gave Adam the power to name everything in creation.
- Naming has power; what we call things or how we think of them has enormous repercussions. The mind is the most potent medicine.
- What we think matters, but we need help. We need help in remembering who we *really* are.

- Broken soundtracks keep us stuck in various states of dis-ease, disease, and sickness.
- The world's economy will be seriously impacted when we wake up and stop hurting ourselves and others. Healthy people do not need medicine or many of the other things big businesses market to us.

The scriptures say, "Awake, O sleeper, and arise from the dead, and Christ will shine on you" (Ephesians 5:14 ESV); healing happens in the light.

We need to hear this call of "Awake, O sleeper." Any belief contrary to the truth—that we are perfectly loved—can cause us to sin (miss the mark) and can put us into a deep sleep—a virtual coma. Christ continually calls us to awaken from the sleep of not knowing who we truly are.

You—yes, *you*—are created in the very image of the Creator. His name says so!

After God showed me the name that He had given me (Grace), like a child, I asked, "What's your name, Papa?" He answered me by showing me this:

Y

H

W

H

This is usually translated as "Yahweh," but this is what God showed me:

His name is written top to bottom—not left to right or right to left but standing up!

Y—like your head with arms raised up over it

H—like your torso

W (or V)—like your groin

H—like your hips and legs

You bear the imprint of the Sacred—of the Divine. Let us have our own *Secret Life of Bees* liberation except ours will not be secret anymore! May we all bear the image of Jesus and know our true worth and identity. May you *bee* well, *bee* whole, and *bee* family—grown-up, badass siblings of Yeshua, Jesus the Christ! Find your "honey in the rock."

Shalom Shalom and *amen* and *amen*!

Psalm of Grace

Praise to You, Creator of the universe, for allowing me to suffer as You allowed this also for Your Son.

For it is in suffering that we are refined, our dross burned off as it is with gold.

For if I am to ever see clearly, and no longer through a glass dimly, You must see in me Your own reflection when You gaze upon my heart.

Like the loaves that Jesus broke, You multiply Your blessings, and so it is with shattered dreams. You return to us Your own beauty from our ashes. Remind me, please, that soap is made from ash and what was soiled, You make clean and wholesome.

Thank You, Father/Mother God, for no man can ever touch the strength that You have given me through Your grace. No man, in this world at least, can know such depths of systemic oppression.

David said so long ago, "Kings of armies quickly go in flight: and the women in the houses make a division of their goods" (Psalm 68).

When all the king's horses and all the king's men exhaust their efforts to put that "Humpty-Dumpty" together again, a circle of sisters, all humble in heart, will march right in and bring Your restoration dream to fruition.

Then all will sing and laugh and dance, for then You shall truly be our one and only King—forever and in all ways!

Printed in the United States
by Baker & Taylor Publisher Services